Take
It
to the
Bridge

For further information and to join the
Take It to the Bridge songwriting community,
please go to tothebridgebook.com.

Steve Dawson
and Mark Caro

Take
It
to the
Bridge

GIA Publications, Inc.
Chicago

UNLOCKING THE GREAT SONGS INSIDE YOU

GIA Publications, Inc.
7404 S. Mason Ave.
Chicago, IL 60638
USA
www.giamusic.com

ISBN: 978-1-62277-211-7
G-9234

Design: Thirst / 3st.com

Printed in the United States of America.

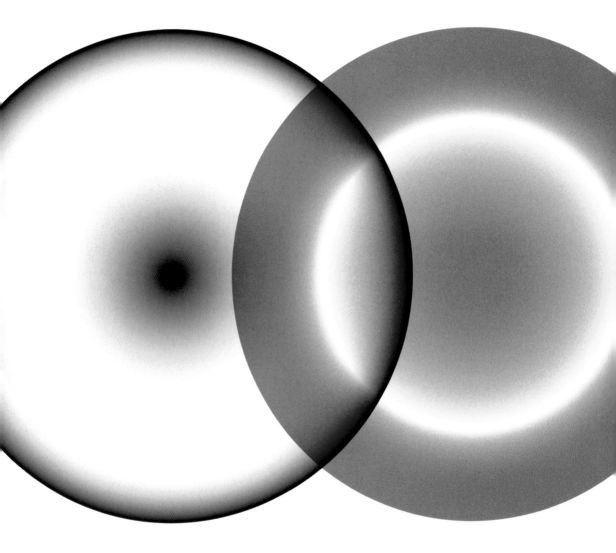

Introductions

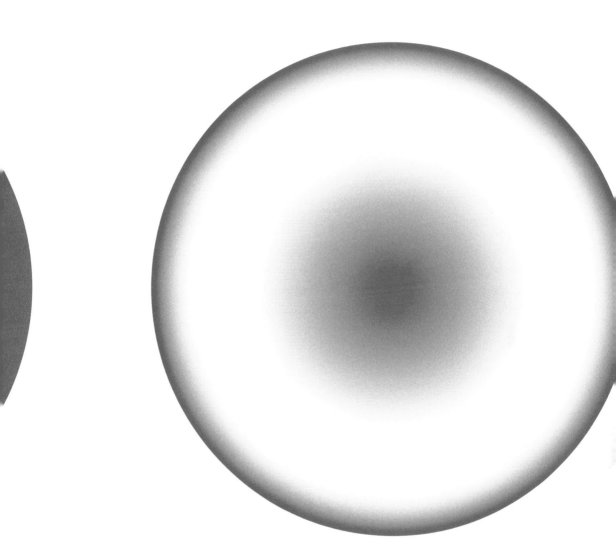

MARK   By the time I signed up to take Steve Dawson's songwriting class at the Old Town School of Folk Music in Chicago, I'd already been a fan of his music — and of him personally — for 20 years. I first heard him sing back in 1989 after I began covering local music for the *Chicago Tribune*. Steve and his soon-to-be wife, Diane Christiansen, were fronting a somewhat twangy group called Stump the Host, and even though I wasn't into music that carried even a hint of country, I developed a band crush.

For one, Steve and Diane had a warm, funny, inviting energy onstage — you enjoyed being in their company as much as you felt they enjoyed being in yours and, especially, each other's. For two, their voices were strong on their own and intoxicating in sweet harmonies. Steve boasted a rich, caramel-flavored tenor that could deliver soul and gospel, country and folk, and rockabilly and straight-up rock with beauty and muscle.

But the main attraction was Steve's songwriting, with some contributions from Diane. I loved the songs. Spanning many genres in a way that felt natural rather than dilettantish, the songs were smart and melodic, surreal and personal, funny as well as tragic in tone. One night in a North Side club, the band debuted a new one called "California Zephyr" that was so catchy, evocative and propulsive, indeed like a locomotive cut loose on the down slope of a mountain, that after the concert I asked Steve and Diane whether I could have the poster board onto which he'd scrawled the lyrics. This, I told them, was their hit record, and I wanted the poster board for posterity. They happily handed it over.

"California Zephyr" did become Stump the Host's first commercial release, a vinyl single put out in 1993 by the local label Minty Fresh. But it also was Stump the Host's only commercial release; the band broke up later that year.

The following year Steve and Diane formed a new band, Dolly Varden, named after a type of trout found in the Pacific Northwest, where Steve had lived before moving to Chicago. No, I wouldn't name a band after a fish that sounds like "Dolly Parton" either, even if that fish got its name from a character in Charles Dickens' novel *Barnaby Rudge*. But bands grow into their names. The players were different but still excellent, and Steve and Diane's singing and songwriting skills continued to blossom along with their special chemistry. More than 20 years later the band remains together, with their sixth album, 2013's *For a While*, earning widespread praise for its emotional depth and melodicism. Its warm reception had the air of a lifetime achievement award, as if there were a collective realization that, hey, these guys have been great for a long time — but as working musicians, not rock stars.

This is to say that Steve, as of this writing, hasn't broken out nationally as I'd thought that he and his band might, and "California Zephyr" isn't a song that everyone from Oregon to Florida knows, although it did also kick off Dolly Varden's second album, *The Thrill of Gravity* (1998), and remains one of their most requested tunes. Steve has had to do what the vast majority of musicians and artists do: work a day job. He toiled at a specialized downtown Chicago record store for a several years, but in 2004 he turned to a field that took greater advantage of his talents: He began teaching guitar at the Old Town School in Chicago's burgeoning Lincoln Square neighborhood.

He was a natural as a teacher because he's patient, sympathetic and knowledgeable, and he takes genuine joy in helping others get in touch with their inner musicality. Soon he was leading songwriting classes as well, coming up with assignments each week to jumpstart students' creative processes.

A few summers ago, I decided I could use that kind of jumpstart and signed up for the class. As someone who had begun many more songs than I'd finished — my imaginary songwriting career consisted mostly of my pulling out my guitar every once in a while to strum chord progressions that I'd made up while I mumbled half-finished lyrics over them — I thought it would be fun and instructive to see what I could produce in a relatively structured environment. Steve would discuss various facets of songwriting each week and give us an assignment that revolved around at least one of them. The following week we'd return with a new song written to Steve's specifications, though he stressed it was better to complete a song that broke the so-called rules than to get hung up on satisfying all of them.

The assignments touched on one or more of the following: form, lyrics, harmony (chords), melody and rhythm. For the first assignment in my session, Steve had us recall a significant friend from childhood and then scribble down key moments that we had shared. He said a song often revolves around just a moment, not a beginning-to-end story, so our task was to write a song springing from one of those moments.

I thought of my childhood best friend John, who lived across the street till he moved to Los Angeles when we were 10, and the time we were horsing around on his top bunk, and he was sitting in front of me leveraging his legs against the bed frame to crush me against the wall. He pushed so hard that he pried the bed away from the wall, and I toppled over backwards with him landing on top of me on the floor. We were resilient little dudes and emerged unscathed. Looking back on that moment, I came up with the phrase, "You're kicking it out from under us."

That, I figured, was the chorus, suggesting perhaps a song about someone about sabotaging a relationship. I let these elements percolate in my mind over the next few days, and the main melodic hook — a doo doo do-do-do thing — came to me as I stepped onto an elevator at work. I figured out the chords on my guitar, wrote down some lyrics, and the next Sunday in class, I nervously played and sang this catchy little pop song for about eight supportive songwriters who were about to unveil musical moments of their own. As someone who had taken years to come up with lyrics for some songs, the experience of crafting within a week a complete song, one that I actually liked, was a revelation.

The following assignment involved writing lyrics chosen solely for the words' sounds, not their meanings, and other exercises called on us to use parallel minor keys, to write a song that would play over a TV-movie scene that Steve had concocted, to follow a strict verse-verse-chorus-verse-chorus-chorus form, to craft a melody using only notes of the pentatonic scale, and to come up with a Monkees song. The class was challenging and fun, and after the eight weeks were over, I had seven new songs.

I took the class again the following summer and wrote more songs that felt good, some completely from scratch, others incorporating elements from previously unfinished songs. Part of what I found fascinating was that each of the eight to 12 people in a class would come up with completely different songs written in their own individual styles and preferred genres. Steve, whose own diverse influences and enthusiasms enable him to embrace a broad spectrum of music, wasn't using his imaginative assignments to teach us to paint by numbers. He was helping us to unlock our creativity, to find our unique voices.

So when Steve asked me about collaborating with him on a book — one that would present a selection of his songwriting assignments and include a broader discussion about the art and craft of composing songs — I jumped at the chance. What follows is literally that: an extended dialogue between Steve, the professional songwriter/ musician, and me, the amateur musician and professional geek who has written a lot about music; and it covers just about every aspect of songwriting we could think of. Do you write lyrics or music first? Do songs have to rhyme? Do you need to know music theory? Should songs actually be about you?

This isn't a textbook. It's a free-flowing conversation between two people who have immersed themselves in music for almost their entire lives and love talking about it. Our hope is that you enjoy reading

He was helping us to unlock our creativity, to find our unique voices.

this the way you might enjoy hanging out with your music-fan friends — and that it inspires you to get the creative gears turning while you explore some of the music we discuss and embark upon crafting your own. Being a good listener should help you become a strong songwriter, and "studying" great songwriting is fun anyway.

Then come the songwriting assignments, a "best of" selection of what has worked in Steve's classes. They cover, as mentioned, form, lyrics, harmony (chords), melody and rhythm, and the occasional wild-card assignment is thrown in there as well. If you're disciplined and knock off one assignment a week — and, sure, you can do that! — you'll have an album's worth of material in a few months. As Steve likes to say: Sweet!

We're also including a number of tables, charts and explanations about various aspects of music theory so you don't feel like you're fumbling in the dark. When I've made up songs, I haven't necessarily been aware of whether I was sticking to one key or modulating all over the place. Working with Steve hasn't made me any less instinctive a songwriter, but I feel now that I have many more tools at my disposal. By the time you're done with this book, you should too.

Songwriting is a mysterious, magical process: some parts inspiration, some parts perspiration. Sometimes the song comes quickly. Sometimes it can be a brutal slog. If writing great songs were simple, more of us would be coming up with — and hearing — more of them.

At the same time, though, *anyone* can write a song. If you want to be a songwriter, you can be a songwriter. The building blocks are simple and within anyone's reach. Heck, when you speak, you're improvising a melody and a rhythm; you're just not self-conscious about it (probably).

So don't get intimidated: You can do this. But don't fool yourself: Songwriting is work, at least if you want it to be any good. It also can be one of the greatest joys imaginable, as you start with nothing and combine words, melody, harmony and rhythm to give birth to something unique and perhaps even beautiful.

There are no strict rules when it comes to songwriting or to using this book. Start with the big dialogue, take note of the song-form descriptions and tables and do the assignments in order — or skip around, find the questions you'd like answered at a given moment, pinpoint the songwriting assignment that fits your particular mood or simply open the book at random intervals to process what's there.

Read on, perhaps with your guitar, piano or other instrument of choice by your side, and get ready to face the music.

STEVE   After I'd been teaching songwriting classes at the Old Town
School of Folk Music in Chicago for a few years — and, by
virtue of some accidental combination of experience and
temperament, was actually having a pretty successful go of
it — students started suggesting I compile of book of the class
writing assignments. I didn't even consider it worth consider-
ing until I read Mark Caro's wonderful book *The Foie Gras Wars*
in 2009. I thought, "A-ha, Mark knows how to write!" Mark and
I have talked about music and songwriting for more than 20
years, and, as he said, he's a songwriter who's been in several
of my classes. I shyly suggested the book idea to Mark, and he
was enthusiastic.

Mark is one of those rare journalists who can convey multiple layers of meaning and details without the results sounding wordy
or labored over. Mark had written for the Chicago Tribune for more than
25 years, first as a music writer profiling local bands (including my first
band, Stump The Host) and more recently as a features writer for the
Arts & Entertainment section, traveling around the world with the
Chicago Symphony Orchestra.

It turns out that Mark's love of songs and the songwriting process is similar to mine, and while we've discussed the art of songwriting,
we have become better friends. I am very grateful he agreed to work
on this book with me, because, honestly, without him it would not exist.

I want to say this before you begin: I don't claim to know how
to teach anybody anything, let alone something so individual and subjective as writing songs. The truth is, dear readers, you already know how
to write songs. You've been, in a sense, studying them your whole life.
My goal as a teacher, and the goal of this book, is to unlock the songs
lurking inside of you. They are in there. I have witnessed the births of
hundreds of songs in my Old Town School of Folk Music classes, some
so beautiful that the class is wiping back tears by the end. These songs
were written by people exactly like you: lovers of music; strummers of
guitars, banjos, mandolins; people who've dreamed of writing songs
like the ones they love. So, welcome and good luck.

As Mark says: You can do this!

The Dialogue

What exactly is inspiration, and how much of songwriting is about getting inspired vs. getting down to work?

STEVE   That's a tough question, because in some ways inspiration is indefinable. The word itself comes from "breath" or breathing in of life. Inspiration is where the good songs come from, and many songwriters, myself included, tend to believe that there is a spiritual element — something beyond the self — going on. Some songs arrive nearly fully formed, as if they were just waiting to be released and I happened to be lucky enough to be there at the right time and place. I think that is the key to it. You have to make yourself available. That means creating time and space to invite inspiration.

That is increasingly difficult in the modern world. To be truly available you have to turn off your cell phone and your computer and any other distractions, find a quiet place where no one can hear you or interrupt you and then be there with your thoughts and whatever musical instrument you play. One tough thing is that you can do all that and still not walk away with anything, and that can build frustration. The truth is, I believe, that every time you commit to making yourself available, you are doing valuable work. Here's a quote from Picasso that is apt: "Inspiration does exist, but it must find you working."

So that's the deal. I find that even if I don't get anything good, at least I'm practicing guitar and working the creative parts of my brain. So, in that respect, the "getting down to work" part is making yourself available. And the tricky thing is that inspiration rarely arrives the same way twice. I've had songs arrive while I'm driving, walking around downtown, waking up in the morning and sitting in a room with my guitar. You can't *make* it happen, but you can increase your chances of having things show up by committing yourself to the idea and making space.

After that, the second process begins: editing, which is very different but equally important.

M   I once heard playwright Tony Kushner say, "Writing is a muscular activity as well as an intellectual activity." As a writer I know this to be true, yet it really struck a chord, so to speak. You can think about a short story/magazine article/novel/play/

screenplay/whatever in your head, but until you sit down with pen and paper — or keyboard and screen — you're not fully engaging the creative process, and you're not getting the work done.

That said, songwriting is different from just about anything else. Sometimes a song comes from meticulous crafting while seated at a piano or strumming a guitar, but sometimes you can work out a lot of it, if not almost the whole thing, in your head — even if it's inevitably transformed once it's performed in the physical world. That's how it has worked with me, at any rate. I may be riding my bike or swimming

"Inspiration does exist, but it must find you working."

or taking a walk, and a song snippet — a little melody, snatch of rhythm, turn of phrase or some combination — may pop into my mind, and I'll repeat it over and over mentally so I don't forget it, at least until I can archive it somehow. If I was carrying my little digital recorder, I'd sing it into that, sometimes making primitive beat-box noises with my mouth. Sometimes I'd call my work Voicemail from my cell phone and mumble the song fragment, hand cupped over mouth so no passersby could hear me. Now I usually use Voice Memos app on my phone.

I had such a moment yesterday morning when I was walking from the train to the office and thinking about my tendency to flit from project to project — or in some friends' cases, profession to profession — without resolving or completing anything. I kept coming back to the phrase "On to the next one, on to the next one …" and as I played it over and over in my head, the words suggested a rhythm, which suggested a beat, which led to some jittery instrumentation (I'm hearing some sort of staccato tremolo effect) and at least one chord change. So maybe it's a chorus in search of a song. I don't know. I sang it into my digital recorder nonetheless. It's a start, and it's easier to build on something than to stare at the proverbial blank page.

That's a case in which words and music arrived together. More often the music comes more naturally for me, and then I have to labor over the words; that becomes the muscular activity, a matter of me and an open notebook. (I find the creativity flows more easily when I'm applying pen to paper and crossing out the terrible lines than when I'm typing onto a screen.) Inspiration for lyrics and inspiration for music may be two different things, no? You like to ask this one in class, so I'll turn the tables:

What generally comes first for you, words or music?

s

I like to say I'll take inspiration any way I can get it. So that means that if a phrase is what kicks things off — great! If it's a chord sequence that suggests a mood or a melody — great! Most often lately it seems to be chords in some order that strike my ears as something interesting or that transport me into a mood or memory. That's the way I'll go if I'm starting with nothing: trying to grab a song out of "thin air."

A couple of songs have come out recently using this method that I'm really happy with. The weird thing, the unexplainable thing, is that words emerged as soon as the chord sequence felt right, and the words spilled out pretty effortlessly. It was as if they were just waiting for me to invite them in — by composing their "theme" music. I wish I could have this happen all the time, but if I *try* to do it, it generally produces nothing worthwhile. The other weird thing is that this has happened not when I planned to write a song but just by chance. I picked up the guitar by habit and started plucking around, intending to just spend a few minutes relaxing with the guitar. And there was the song. Examples from my song catalog that appeared this way would be "Long Overdue," "In The Valley Of The Whale," "Simple Pleasure," "Obsidian," "Mastodons," "Ezra Pound and the Big Wood River," "Mayfly" and lots of others.

This is still in the "inspiration" category, not the "editing" category. All my songs get a thorough "going over" after the inspiration phase — where I play around with word choices, rhymes, re-harmonization, writing additional verses (if necessary), choice of key, melodic variation and form. That can all go on in my head almost anywhere and anytime. I work on editing all the time. Ah, but I'm off topic!

On the rare occasion that I come up with a lyric phrase that feels like a good idea for a song, it can make the process easier and less up to chance. The words in the phrase often suggest how the song will sound: fast, slow, major key, minor key? Phrases that have launched songs for me include "I'm the one I despise," "mouthful of lies," "today she found the way to break my heart" and "preaching to the choir." With "I'm the one I despise," I thought of that line somewhere along the way and laughed out loud. It is a funny line, but it also has a lot of truth in it, and it's something I can relate to, and I think others can, too. Those are very important qualities in a "phrase"-based song, I think. This is also the way most country songs are written, I think, and I recall reading in Keith Richards' book, *Life*, that he said that a good phrase is songwriting gold and gets the whole thing focused.

So I had the phrase and immediately got to work. I set it to music and a tempo and got to thinking what could rhyme with "despise." I didn't want to use obvious rhymes. Interesting rhymes would make for a better payoff. I ended up with, "All along I thought it was you, but now I realize" in Verse 1, and "Looking through this list of things I used to criticize" in Verse 2. That took lots and lots of walking around and thinking about words and ideas that both fit the topic and kept the mood right. I'm thinking it was weeks of work; I don't recall exactly. That's all song-craft work, not inspiration work. The inspiration was strictly the phrase itself; everything else — the chords, the tune, the rest of the lyrics, the form — was constructed using the tools I've accumulated from writing songs for 30 years.

Some of my students will write an entire lyric first before adding any music. Some people will "free" write or use journaling to explore thoughts, poems, images and stories before involving music. This can be an effective way of unlocking the creative imagination. In class I always recommend a great book by Natalie Goldberg called *Writing Down The Bones* that beautifully explores, in an inspiring and approachable way, this type of creative exploration through words.

Personally, I tend to think that the songs that arrive "music first," from the first process described above, are more soulful or "real" somehow. That unexplainable arrival is pretty magical and awesome and makes the song carry that magic with it. The more crafted songs, the "phrase first" songs, to me, feel more "of this earth" and often have a level of cleverness that I don't completely trust.

M Funny that you should mention cleverness, because I've grown quite wary and weary of that quality myself. When I was younger, I really used to revel in puns and witticisms in songs. I think the intended dynamic is: Hey, they're so smart making that joke, and I'm so smart in getting it—yay, us! The wordplay in Elvis Costello and the Attractions' *Get Happy!!* is so rapid-fire and dense that I'd get happy parsing lines such as "Check your effects and check your reflection/I'm so affected in the face of your affection." Actually, I still love that album, in part because Costello's delivery is so urgent and impassioned, and the Attractions are so committed and nimble, that I accept the cleverness as a byproduct of his raging psyche. But a few albums later when he was singing about putting "the numb into number and the cut into cutie... the slum into slumber and the boot into beauty," I cringed at the cutesy self-consciousness.

The problem with cleverness is that it's often cold, like a shield against revealing true emotions. This is why my appreciation for a band such as They Might Be Giants never gets past a certain point; I appreciate the catchiness and smarts but usually from a distance. Music, poetry, powerful emotions — they stand up to repeated listenings, the experience growing deeper along the way. Cleverness — not so much. How often do you listen to even the best comedy albums?

All that said, I've written a whole bunch of songs that fall into the category of so-called funny ones. The first song I ever wrote was a doo-woppy thing called "The Red, White and Blues" that went like this: "My baby shot me in the arm/Now I'm red, I'm white and I'm bluuuuuuue." My friend Stu and I long ago made up a song called "You've Got the Heart of an Artichoke (and a Head of Lettuce)" that was, yes, a series of vegetable puns: "We tried to get by on my celery... You didn't carrot all...Olive you." I have one old song, "I'd Like To Borrow a Girl," that revolves around library/book jokes ("I want to check her *out!*") and another, "Basa," that descends into sausage puns ("All I wanna do is...Kill Basa!"). Perhaps the pinnacle (or nadir) of this sort of thing is one called "My Heart's a Sheep (and It's Bleating for You)," which contains the couplet "While I kept hoping it would get better and better/You took the strings of my heart and knitted a sweater." It fades out to cries of "Baa baa love." So, *mea culpa.*

But I consider these novelty tunes, not attempts to write serious songs. You're talking about a more insidious form of cleverness. But the simple fact, for me at least, is that even when I'm not trying to be jokey, I often find it easier to be clever than to find words that fit whatever intangible mood I think I'm creating through the music. I wish I had an app that would allow me to download that feeling into the song. Instead I'm sitting there with my pen and paper trying to come up with a line and a rhyme, and this can feel like an intellectual activity, like you're trying to *solve* the song. At times it's probably better to abandon the search for that perfect rhyme, because when you nail it, you might feel...clever. Yet I'm fairly anal about rhyming, too.

So this all raises some questions:

How do you create songs about feelings and emotions without letting your head get in the way? And: How do you decide when it's OK to rhyme or not to rhyme?

S   I don't disparage people who are able to write great "clever" songs, Elvis Costello included. John Prine, and in a lot of cases, John Lennon as well, wrote great songs that are more about clever wordplay than heartfelt sentiment. It's a rare gift to be able to combine playful and witty language with deeper meaning. When it works it's fantastic. You have a brain for language and double-meanings, etc. I wouldn't discount that. Those funny songs *are* funny, and that's great. I don't have that kind of brain, though, so for me it sounds forced. If it sounds forced, it doesn't work at all; in fact, it does the opposite and draws attention to its awkwardness.

Rhyming, to me, depends on the context of the song. I can get very obsessive about rhymes if it's a song that feels like it has to have exact rhymes. More and more I'm trying to write without thinking about what I'm writing, trying to disengage any sort of qualifying about what's being said or how it's being presented. This, of course, is nearly impossible. The goal is to have the words "write themselves" and to get out of the way. I find that this happens in short bursts. In between bursts I'm trying to re-play the chords, re-sing the words that have just appeared and trying to stay within the mood they've created. The words are all certainly from *me* and about *me*, but they are from a place that's deeper (I hope) than trying to express how I'm feeling.

This is all very esoteric, I know. I've read interviews with Paul Simon, Neil Young and Bob Dylan where they all express, in their own ways, this same process. The goal is to get out of the way and take down what's appearing without judging it. Often the words show up with some rhyming because that is a part of the musicality of language. I love the *sound* of words — the rhythms and spaces, the common vowels and consonants, hard sounds and soft sounds. In a lot of ways writing lyrics, for me, is finding the musicality of the words and playing with the patterns. So if the mood created is right and the words sound good and musical, the meaning is secondary. Rhyme is part of the musicality. And that would include near rhymes and internal rhymes, even just common occurring vowel sounds inside a line.

You've hit upon what makes songwriting so exciting and daunting at the same time: So much is about feel, not formula. There are songs that I love, and I have little clue what they're about. The combination of words and music make me feel a certain way, and I don't need to retreat into my head to analyze it all. It's like when Lennon convinced Paul McCartney not to cut the line "The movement you need is on your shoulder" from "Hey Jude." McCartney, who's never been too rigorous in demanding deep meanings from every line, thought that one made no sense, but it spoke to Lennon, it stayed in, and it feels right.

McCartney's "Jet" is a great song as well as a load of nonsense. So be it. The lyrical content feels less than essential in that one, as opposed to, say, "Imagine," which is a beautiful melody nonetheless driven by the words. It's almost like there are two categories of songs: those in which the lyrics matter and those in which they don't.

Hmm. Let me refine that. The lyrics of "Jet" matter in terms of how they sound and the images they convey and the way they add to the song's exuberance. But they're working on that level of what you just called "the musicality of language." That's a different approach from songwriters who focus on what they want a song to *say* first and foremost. The early R.E.M. albums were more driven by the musicality of Michael Stipe delivering lyrics that you could barely understand yet were richly evocative in their phrasings and imagery. Later-period R.E.M. was more about the songs' *meaning*.

But let's get back to the rhymes, because those rules sure feel slippery. Writing lyrics offers more freedom than writing poetry because you can change so much with the delivery. You can stretch one syllable to three ("I lo-o-ove you") or compress a lot of verbiage into a tight space to keep to the rhythm. Also, a lot of in-the-ballpark rhymes are commonly accepted, like "alone" with "home."

Yet some folks get away with more than others. I always thought Sam Cooke was pushing it rhyming "slacks," "back" and "like" (pronounced "lak") in "Twistin' the Night Away," though none of that has interfered with that song's classic status. And I'll take those rhymes over the Steve Miller Band's rhyming of "Texas" with the ungrammatical "facts is," "justice" and "taxes" in "Take the Money and Run." Now *there's* one of those lyrics-don't-matter songs; you have to actively suppress processing its content to enjoy its catchiness. Then there's the vexing way Annie Lennox pronounces "this" as "these" so it can match up with "disagree," "seas" and "something" in "Sweet Dreams (Are Made of This)."

It's much simpler to take the John Mellencamp route and rhyme "small town" with "small town" more than a dozen times in, yes, "Small Town." Yet as much as I've made fun of that song, I can't deny that it works — and I can't see it being better if he'd rolled out a litany of "down," "gown," "frown," "noun" and "clown."

Does it all come down to the gut check?

S   Yeah, "Small Town" is a song that shouldn't work. It should be totally annoying to listen to. Yet, it not only works, it's very powerful. It's like a chant or something. I saw Mellencamp perform that on Elvis Costello's TV show *Spectacle* on a song-writers' circle with Kris Kristofferson and a bunch of other great songwriters. He started "Small Town," and I thought: Uh, oh, this could go very badly. But I'll be dammed if that wasn't a highlight of the show.

I think one reason is that he means it completely. For him that song is the truth, and that, I think, is more important than anything we've discussed so far. If a song connects with a shared human truth, it will hit home "in the gut," which is immediate, before the thought process can get involved and start qualifying. That's where chills come from. Not many songs get to that point. Mellencamp wrote that one direct from a truth in his life and heart, and it comes through.

I think all songwriters are trying to find the songs that will hit home that way, but there's certainly no method of doing that. My guess is he picked up a guitar and started singing that song pretty much as you hear it now. It was immediate. If you are lucky enough to come up with a song that has that embedded truth and immediacy, you might think: Ah, I've figured it out, I'll just write like this all the time, and they'll all come out this way! But, of course, they won't. The pool is forever changing.

The subjects of rhyming and lyrical clarity are interesting. It really depends on the style of music you're writing for, I think. In country music the meaning has to be crystal clear, and the rhymes have to be both sonically pleasing and not boring. It's really, really hard to write good, concise country songs. The level of songcraft in country songs is very high, much higher than in the rock and singer/songwriter worlds. By songcraft I mean economy of language, rhyming, verse structure, melodic and harmonic development and certainly storytelling. The craft in Nashville is staggering, and the competition is fierce. The trouble is that music is a business first there, so the writers are constantly refer-encing current hits to try and write new hits. That makes for a sort of circular firing squad thing where all the songs end up having the same overall attitude and musical cadences.

Rock and singer/songwriter songs tend to have more flexibility in their lyrical conciseness, which I prefer personally, but it makes for a lot of very lazy writing. Bob Dylan opened a door by expanding the subject matter of songs and by introducing boldly non-linear, impressionistic language, but it was also a Pandora's box. There's lots of truly horrible lyric writing that gets qualified, and often praised, as "artsy" or "poetic." I'm not gonna name any names here, but I think you probably could come up with a list without trying too hard.

On the other hand, I recently heard an old Joni Mitchell song, "Cactus Tree," that'd I'd not heard before. Holy crap, she is an amazing writer. The sound of the language, the consistency of the imagery, the emotional weight are sustained throughout. Staggering. I find I take writers like her for granted. I know a good number of her songs very well, so it was nice to hear a song I'd never heard before and be floored by it.

That should be the goal for "poetic" writing! Can it stand up to the Joni Test? Or the "Visions of Johanna"/Dylan Test?

Rhyming in songs reached its peak in the 1920s and '30s, actually, with Lorenz Hart, Cole Porter, Ira Gershwin and other writers for Broadway and Hollywood. The wordplay and internal rhyming was taken to its fullest fruition in those songs and hasn't been topped. Dylan has

Our collective cultural listening is moving away from the need to have perfect rhymes.

said that he put an end to Tin Pan Alley because songwriting had to go somewhere else; that type of songwriting had moved beyond its peak. (Later he would record albums of Tin Pan Alley covers.) Dylan himself often has pretty strict rhyming in his songs, sometimes to the point of being distracting. But he's so good at using interesting words to surround the destination rhyming word that it doesn't matter.

It seems to me that our collective cultural listening is moving away from the need to have perfect rhymes, even moving away from the need to have any kind of end rhymes at all. I think hip hop has made this happen more than anything else. It's all about near rhymes and common vowels and consonants in close proximity and rhythmic symmetry. That has spilled over into all forms of music now. It may be weird for folks in our 40s or older to accept, but anyone younger than us has grown up with a steady diet of hip hop. It is ingrained in the mainstream culture. Words are chosen for their rhythmic interplay and sonic connection as much as for their meaning, and end rhymes are sounding more and more "old fashioned." We've been slowly weaned off the need to hear rhymes all the time in songs, so a non-rhymed verse goes by pretty smoothly. I think that's progress. A finite number of words rhyme in the English language, and most of the best rhyming happened 70 years ago!

For me, I'm a fan of vowel-sound connections; a common long "a" or "o" in two words or phrases is enough of a connection most of the time. For the record I've always hated the Eurythmics' "Sweet Dreams" because of the "this/disagree/seas" thing. She has to purposefully mispronounce the word "this" to make the sonic connection with "disagree," and to me that is bad writing (and it sounds stupid).

Of course, that was a massive hit and continues to be played and enjoyed worldwide, so what do I know? Proof that the words barely matter in pop music — if they matter at all. "Jet" is another great example of that. It's better *not* to know the words to "Jet." When someone told me that it was about McCartney's dog, I wished I could go back in time and skip hearing that fact.

M Wait, what? "Jet" is about his dog? OK, I just checked this out, and Jet was *thought* to be the name of his black Labrador, but he said in a 2010 interview that it *actually* was the name of his pony. Feel better?

Really, though, it doesn't matter which animal was Jet, because if it had been named Snugglebumps, he wouldn't have used it. "*Jet!*" is just a great thing to shout in an arena-friendly rocker, and I can't see any critter connection to that business about the major being a lady *suffragette!* I'd guess he used the word/name as a way to start the song and then let the creative process take over, leaving behind no traces of an animal or, for that matter, an air-transportation vehicle.

This actually could be a good exercise to assign: Write a song that revolves around a word or name that has little or nothing to do with the rest of the song's content. The downside is you might wind up with another "Sussudio."

Oh, and for what it's worth, McCartney also named the same-era song "Helen Wheels" for his land rover, and, of course, "Martha My Dear" *is* about his sheepdog.

As for the Joni and "Visions of Johanna" Tests, those are mighty high bars you're raising for so-called poetic writing. But I get your point: If you're going to aspire to poetry in songwriting, you'd better come close to the mark, because when you miss it, the landing is painful. Silly rhymes are more forgivable than pretentiousness. I often can tune out insubstantial lyrics if I'm enjoying the music, but sometimes a phrase hits me the wrong way, like a reference to "the smell of hospitals in winter," and I rebel.

I don't want to admire lyrics; I want to be moved by them. One songwriter who leaves me awestruck in his ability to marry precise, potent words to instantly timeless melodies and stunningly expressive playing is Richard Thompson. His lyrics aren't fancy, yet they capture worlds in their imagery and insights. "Beeswing," for instance, is a heartbreaker conveying a man's sorrowful admiration for a lost love who proved too free-spirited and self-destructive for him. The key line is simple yet devastating: "She was a rare thing/Fine as a bee's wing." Likewise, his great motorcycle ballad "1952 Vincent Black Lightning" rises to the level of poetry through the crispness and evocative power of his observations: "Red hair and black leather, my favorite color scheme" or the plainly observed "But he smiled/ To see her cry." You don't need to be a James Joyce aficionado to appreciate that — and Thompson was more than 20 years into his career when he wrote those songs, so sustaining inspiration doesn't have to be a problem.

Thompson, Mitchell and Dylan came out of the folk tradition, with which I know you're well acquainted. How much of a defining factor is that?

Also, many of their songs have a narrative arc; the traditional folk ballad is like a short story. So here's a question for you:

What percentage of your songs are about *you* and what *you're feeling* as opposed to a scenario you've concocted or characters you're inhabiting?

S   This is a tricky question because so much of my writing is a mix of real things that have actually happened jumbled up with made-up stuff. I think I'm not alone in writing this way. In most interviews I read with songwriters, they describe this similar mix of fact and fiction. Some writers do seem to

write primarily through the voices of characters: John Prine,
Joe Henry and Robbie Robertson would be examples of
people who do this very well. Some writers write primarily
through personal experience in a confessional sort of way:
Joni Mitchell, Jackson Browne, post-1967 John Lennon and
Conor Oberst would be examples. I tend to lean toward the
confessional "school."

Generally my songs start with a memory or thought from my
own life that has some emotional tug, and then I take it from there. I
often end up with a mix of some actual, factual stuff and then flesh out
the lyrics with some made-up imagery based on the sound of the words,
the rhyming (if there is rhyming) and whatever my imagination offers up.
In classes I often cite poet Richard Hugo saying you have no obligation
to the *facts*, but you have absolute obligation to the *truth*. The truth
would be the emotional heart and soul of the song — what the song is
really about; what the song is trying to put across. The actual facts are
unimportant, generally, unless you're writing a fact-based story song
like "The Wreck of the Edmund Fitzgerald," but the truth is absolute.
You must write from and for the truth, or your song won't have any real
impact. This can be done through a character's voice or through your
own voice. If you conjure fictional images to support the truth of the
song, that's just fine.

I read an interview with Joni Mitchell where she said that she
made a conscious decision sometime in the late '60s to write absolutely
from her own life in a very personal way as a sort of challenge to her
listeners — to see how far she could go and still maintain an audience. In
her case it made her audience love her more. A lot of people find the confessional approach to be off-putting. The slew of '70s singer-songwriters
from James Taylor to Dan Fogelberg really turned some people off to the
idea of rock stars singing sensitive songs about their oversensitive selves.
I certainly get that, and the world was saturated with treacly songs in the
'70s, and the image of a lone singer with an acoustic guitar will forever
carry the baggage of all those songs. Even so, I am still moved the most
by a song that has a personal connection to the writer. I think there's a
bigger context and more at risk for the writer and in turn for the listener.

In my formative years, when I was a sensitive teen, I found those
records — by Neil Young, Jackson Browne, Joni Mitchell, Van Morrison,
Paul Simon and many others — to be a place of real solace and a way
of understanding things. They gave me context and comfort for the
emotions I was grappling with and, I think, made me a better person.
When I write I try to remember how those records made me feel, and I

proceed from a place with that kind of understanding. I've tried to write through characters with little success. I think it's a different mindset.

Most songwriters, even the most confessional, have written character songs. James Taylor, the "king" of the confessional singer-songwriters, has a handful of great ones, including a song called "Millworker," written in the voice of a young woman working in a textile mill. Dylan, who, for better or for worse, basically created the singer-songwriter genre, has written brilliant songs through the voices of characters and brilliant songs in first person based on life experience and brilliant songs that are a big jumble of real-life events and thoughts, imagination and wordplay. In interviews he is, of course, elusive about the sources of his material, so we can only guess what is fact and what is fiction in many of his songs.

Bruce Springsteen is one of the best character writers, I'd say. A lot of his big, epic songs are like short stories set to music. He really gets to the heart of the characters and brings you into the drama. I think a lot of his own life experiences are mixed into those characters' stories. I read an interview with him where he was asked about how much of his own life is in those songs, and he said, basically, that the names have been changed to protect the innocent. He also has a handful of very moving confessional songs.

I think it's up to every songwriter to explore both ways of writing and to find what works best for themselves. I try to assign at least one character-writing assignment each session in my classes. A somewhat morbid but effective approach is to go through the obituaries and write a song about someone who's passed away. The obituary will give you a brief outline of a person's life, and you can fill in the details with your imagination.

M See, this is an area where our approaches differ, because I tend to look at my lyrics from the standpoint of character first — like who is this person singing this song, and what is he (or she) feeling? That person *may* be me, or it may be some variation of me, or it may be someone completely different, but my default is that the "I" of a song is not "I, Mark Caro." There's probably some defensive/self-protective aspect in there, like I don't want listeners assuming that I'm writing my autobiography musically, but it's also because I don't want the song to be restricted to my own spectrum of emotions and experiences. As in my work at the newspaper, I think my subjects are more interesting than the guy doing the writing. In practice this often is a matter of where the song comes from.

One song I wrote for your class, "Dunno," began with that word repeated several times to make up the chorus. Now I needed the rest of the song, so I had to think: Who would say "Dunno" over and over and why? I decided it was a guy who'd been treating his girlfriend poorly, and when she'd ask why he was doing what he was doing, he'd shrug and say, "Dunno." So the guy was kind of a jerk — *not like me at all*, you see. He was also self-aware enough to note: "Why would I say/Such a wretched thing?/I say…'Dunno, dunno, dunno…'" My task was to be true to this particular voice, not my own feelings on how one should strive to be an open communicator with one's love partner. The same was true for a song I wrote a while back called "My Baby's Got Issues." Who would say that, and what kind of issues might *he* have?

To me the master of character songwriters is Randy Newman. He's like the anti-James Taylor, although he did enlist a good-humored Taylor to sing the cocky Lord part on his *Faust* musical soundtrack. Newman inhabits all sorts of negative figures — "rogues" is the term often bandied about — yet rarely does he appear to condescend to them. Even the bigoted narrator of "Rednecks," as bold and complex a piece of social satire as you'll ever hear — as it skewers both Southern racism and Northern hypocrisy while employing the N-word liberally — is given a specific point of view. That whole album, *Good Old Boys*, is filled with desperate, troubled characters who stir sympathy amid beautiful melodies and arrangements, even as these folks sometimes also provoke laughs, such as the poor soul in "A Wedding in Cherokee County" who laments, "Why must everybody laugh at my mighty sword?" Newman's previous album, *Sail Away*, begins with a majestic sales pitch to Africans to board a slave ship, and it ends with God devastatingly pondering what dupes people are to believe in Him.

Newman, especially in his earlier works, is the counterargument to my earlier anti-cleverness stance. I *do* get repeated enjoyment out of a funny song such as "Political Science." I think the key is that Newman isn't taking emotional shortcuts in his satire; it's driven by genuine anger, despair, amusement, bewilderment, empathy and a whole host of other feelings. And the music makes the case as much as the lyrics.

What Newman is doing is very different from what Joni Mitchell is doing — or Frank Ocean or Metallica, for that matter — yet it all falls under a common umbrella. So let's get to a basic question:

32   What is a song anyway?

Is it a story? A captured moment? A feeling? A plea or declaration? An extended metaphor? A memory? A collage of words and images? A therapy session? A mere vessel to carry you through some music?

Granted, it can be any and all of these things, but how do you approach this? As you move through life, what's the tipping point where you think: This feeling I'm having, this dynamic I'm observing, this memory I'm reliving isn't just food for thought — it's a *song*?

S   A very good bunch of questions. I was just reading a re-printed interview with Bob Dylan (in *American Songwriter*) where he talks about how there are different types of songs just like there are different types of people — an infinite variety covering everything from folk ballads to classical pieces. If you think about it, the works of everyone from Dylan to Lady Gaga, from Hank Williams to Jay-Z, from Jobim to Kurt Weill...they're all *songs*. So what do they have in common? Words set to music.

The most common subject by *far* is love — seeking it, celebrating it or suffering the loss of it. Something about music and words together creates the canvas for romantic musings. Lyrics that are on the "poetic" side come from the long tradition of the balladeer, I believe. The fella with the lute going from town to town singing songs of love and tragedy. Storytelling and romance. I've always heard that *The Iliad* and *The Odyssey* were originally sung, though I guess some scholars disagree.

Storytelling and music, I would propose, go back to before the written word existed. It is a primal thing. But equally as important is music for celebration and dancing. That is the main split, I think: songs of narrative and songs for dancing and celebration. Pop music usually is a combination of the two, with an emphasis on the dance. Folk music is usually more about the narrative and what the song is trying to say.

Rock? It depends. Knowing the words to Little Richard's songs isn't of any importance for your enjoyment, but Chuck Berry's lyrics are brilliantly crafted and add to the experience. McCartney, I would say, is constantly toying with this balance ("Jet" vs. "Eleanor Rigby"), being a fan of both artists/approaches. In his book *Chronicles*, Dylan talks about how truly weird the words and stories to lots of old folk songs are, and that gave him a sense of freedom to write and explore anything. He was also inspired by actual Beat poets in New York at the time: Allen Ginsberg, etc.

So where does that put me? I, like, most narrative-based singer-songwriters, have a preponderance of slow, melancholy songs with dense lyrics. We're either asked, or we wonder to ourselves, "What is the matter with you? Why can't you write any happy songs?" It's because of the tradition I'm aligned with, mostly. I'm not a sad sack in my life, but I love music that explores and expresses the darker emotions and the melancholy. When you set it to a beat it becomes R&B, soul, bluegrass...etc.

Richard Thompson is one of the absolute best writers of the narrative-based song. He's poetic without being showy, and emotion is always at the forefront without being melodramatic. Brilliant. And his songs, for the most part, are tragic and dark and very, very sad. He offers no apology for this. Patty Griffin, I'm told, was berated by people

There aren't that many purely happy songs. Think about it.

telling her to write a "happy" song, so she wrote "Heavenly Day," which is about spending a day with her dog, though she never says that outright in the lyrics. Impending doom is hovering all around that song, though. The heavenly day is a respite from the bitter reality of life. So that's her "happy" song.

I have on occasion made myself write "happy" songs. "I Come To You" (from Dolly Varden's *The Dumbest Magnets*) and "Everything" (from DV's, *The Panic Bell*) are two examples. You've commented on the strangeness of "Everything." I agree. "I Come to You" is probably a better example of a pure, upbeat pop song. It is very, very simple: three two-line verses and a single-line chorus that repeats. "Everything" is basically a big upbeat chorus (again, one phrase broken into pieces and repeated: formula exposed!) with some really weird verses. How did that happen? I had the chorus for a while and needed some verses. That is the best I came up with.

I like both of those songs, but I don't consider them my best work at all. People ask for them at every Dolly Varden show, though, and that is the power of the "happy" song. People *want* to feel good. There aren't that many purely happy songs. Think about it.

My best work, I think, comes from somewhere else. I don't have a mental conversation that determines whether what I'm doing is "a song" or "not a song." Not at the beginning, at least. I'll pick up the guitar, and the something seems to be there waiting for me to play and to sing it. I have no idea how that happens. I long for it to happen, and when it does it always catches me by surprise. If I find myself in that situation, I try my best to stay with it and not to mess it up. Most often those songs start with guitar chords in a progression, then a melody, then lyrics — but all tripping over each other on their way out into the world. I can't clearly remember many of the Stump the Host songs being written; it was so long ago. I do think "10,000 Pounds" came out this way.

They all have images from my memory and life and a sense of loneliness and redemption in the lyrics. That's as much as I can tell you, really. I do go over them after the initial inspiration and play around with the structure and add words if needed, maybe add a chord or sometimes change a key. I've found that it's best mostly to leave them alone, though, as I have occasionally ruined a song with too much tinkering.

M Now you've got me thinking about the whole happy/sad song divide. Not to fixate on the Beatles or anything, but some of their early songs aren't merely happy; they're exuberant: "She Loves You" ("Yeah! Yeah! Yeah!"), "I Want To Hold Your Hand" ("And when I touch you I feel happy inside"), "I'm Happy Just To Dance with You," "I Feel Fine" and so on. Compare those to weightiness of McCartney's towering late-period singles "Hey Jude" ("Take a sad song and make it better") and "Let It Be" ("When I find myself in times of trouble…"). Or consider the relative chirpiness of Lennon's early plea for a girlfriend to "Please Please Me" vs. the desperation of his later "I Want You (She's So Heavy)" — and he grew even darker on his solo debut *Plastic Ono Band*, essentially the prototype for singer-songwriters' painfully confessional albums.

Of course, the Beatles provide lots of middle ground, too, never more jarringly than Lennon crying for "Help!" in the midst of his band's rousing gallop through the song. Likewise, "Getting Better" comes on as infectiously optimistic, but how sunny can a song be that talks about beating a woman and keeping "her apart from the things that she loved"? As you pointed out with Patty Griffin, sometimes the tension between the surface message and undercurrents can give a song extra resonance.

Happy songs can get a fair amount of grief. Katrina and the Waves' "Walking on Sunshine," for example, seems more ridiculed than celebrated these days, yet that's a great pop single with a powerhouse vocal; I think people find such uninhibited peppiness to be embarrassing. The most reviled song in the R.E.M. catalog may be the uncharacteristically chirpy "Shiny Happy People," yet when I first heard it, it didn't strike me as a happy song. I took the narrator to be on the outside looking longingly at the title characters the way Woody Allen gazes at the party train on the opposite track in *Stardust Memories*. Alas, the shiny, happy video didn't convey the same idea.

There are many other examples of a song's form being in deliberate conflict with the content; this could be another good songwriting exercise. Bruce Springsteen's "Born in the U.S.A." on the surface is an anthemic chest-thumper, hence its misguided embrace by Ronald Reagan and fellow conservatives at the time of its 1984 release. Yet it's really an anguished cry about patriotism amid the lingering effects of the Vietnam War. The fierce funk of Sly and the Family Stone's groundbreaking 1969 single "Thank You (Falettinme Be Mice Elf Again)" masks some awfully dark lyrics about facing down a gun-wielding devil. When the band slowed the groove to an ominous thump and Stone drawled the same lyrics in a drugged-out haze two years later on "Thank You for Talkin' To Me Africa," the capper to the battle-scarred classic *There's a Riot Goin' On*, the result was near terrifying.

Sly and the Family Stone could be the poster children for that happy-to-sad progression. The titles on their 1970 greatest-hits compilation would work as chapters of a modern self-help book: "I Want To Take You Higher," "Everybody Is a Star," "Stand!", "Life," Fun," "You Can Make It If You Try," "Dance to the Music," "Everyday People," "Hot Fun in the Summertime," "M'Lady," "Sing a Simple Song," "Thank You (Falettinme Be Mice Elf Again)." Then came *There's a Riot Goin' On* to slam the door on 1960s optimism.

This brings me to your distinction between songs of narrative and songs for dancing and celebration. It's a logical, smart notion that I never considered — that some songs are meant strictly for listening and some for moving. Yet so much of what I listen to falls into the gray area. Rock/soul/R&B/reggae/ska by nature demands a physical response. The drums and beat may not drive you to the dance floor, but they do *something* that inspires an impulse that goes beyond the repose you'd bring to, say, reading poetry. So Marvin Gaye's "What's Going On" and "Mercy Mercy Me (The Ecology)" serve as passionate pleas to heal societal divisions and the environment, respectively, but they also sport seductively fluid grooves that impel you, at the very least, to nod to the rhythm. Many of those Sly and the Family Stone songs also straddle the narrative/dance divide, as do Bob Marley's output, the Rolling Stones' "Street Fighting Man," the Beatles' "Revolution," those Chuck Berry songs you mentioned and many more. There's a reason, aside from economics and general fan disregard, that most rock clubs make you stand. This music expects you to *do* something.

As you said, you've written a lot of slow, melancholy songs with dense lyrics, though I think that description undersells you. My resistance to many singer-songwriters stems from a general lack of melody and musical innovation; the settings often take too much of a backseat to the lyrics for my taste. But you've got a beautiful ear for melody and keen sense of a song's dynamics, as well as an innate soulfulness. You also have your share of musically upbeat songs; you just don't tend to turn them into occasions for dancing and celebration.

"Dangerously Thin," for example, has some propulsion behind it, and if you'd called it, say, "Slammin' Body," you might've gotten the party-hardy types onto the dance floor. "California Zephyr" is a carefully crafted narrative, but it moves like that train you're evoking; I'm not the only one who has bounced around to that one. And, yes, "Everything" is a strange song: It bursts out of the gates with rolling drums and a bold, declarative chorus ("Everything is better… Everything is better when you are around!") before slowing down for

Songs of narrative and songs for dancing and celebration

a minor-key verse with unusual changes, revving back up for the chorus, hitting the brakes for another verse and then veering off into a twinkling detour that, with its sweet harmonies and what sounds like a harpsichord, is reminiscent of the Beach Boys' psychedelic period. That last part could be the middle eight before you slam everything home with that killer chorus again, but instead it's a sweet coda on which the song fades out. Mind you, I don't consider "strange" to be an insult; most of my favorite songs are strange on some level, including some that became huge commercial hits, such as the Beach Boys' "Good Vibrations." I'm just noting that even when you were setting out to write a happy song, you found ways to upend listener expectations and to complicate the celebratory vibe.

Finding the right setting for a song seems a tricky business. The Beatles sped up their initial, slower takes of "Please Please Me" and "Revolution." Glenn Tilbrook has said Squeeze didn't find that deliberate, sinuous beat of "Tempted" until the band reapproached the song with producer Elvis Costello after recording a poppier version with Dave Edmunds. Those were wise decisions. I'm a primitive guitar player, and my internal metronome tends to rush, so when I make up a song, it often gets faster the more I play it. Is that a good choice for the song? Sometimes. Perhaps sometimes not.

How do you decide how much you want listeners to groove or to rock out to what you're saying?

How do you weigh the relationship between a song's content and its musical setting?

Do you see them as basically harmonious, or do you try to create a certain kind of tension?

S   Humans respond immediately to rhythm. I've read that the response to rhythm occurs in the brain stem while other elements of music are perceived in more "evolved" brain locations. Did you read Daniel J. Levitin's *This is Your Brain on Music*? It's generally a fascinating book, with some flaws but overall really interesting, about how the brain processes all the elements of music: rhythm, melody, harmony, dynamics, repetition and more. It gets very scientific, but I did take away some good stuff. I realized that I hadn't been paying enough attention to the groove of my songs. Now I do.

If the rhythm is not happening, you'll have a very hard time engaging listeners. Keep their toes tapping, and they'll listen to anything. Your song must have a solid rhythmic groove or "feel," whether it's solo acoustic folk, rock, speed metal, Latin jazz, disco or anything else. The other thing I learned is that playing music works nearly your entire brain; all the different areas of your brain have to cross-communicate constantly to process the complexities of playing a piece of music, and that increases when you sing. So we're really giving our brains some great exercise when we sing and play songs. Nice!

Still, I have to push myself to think about the underlying pulse, feel and propulsion of a song, given that I am so drawn to words, melody and chords. I've noticed this more since I've been producing recordings for others and paying attention to great records from all eras. This can be more of a "production" consideration than a "songwriting" consideration. A really well-written song can usually stand up to different musical surroundings and still work. Some songwriters consider that the test of a great song. That's an old-fashioned view, from the Tin Pan Alley era, but still something you hear. That would mean instrumentation, dynamics, rhythmic feel, gender of vocalist and maybe even time signature all could change, and the song still would hit the mark.

I don't mean to keep going back to Dylan, but I happen to be in a bit of a Dylan phase right now. He was asked in an interview why he is constantly changing how he plays and sings his classic songs while many of his contemporaries from the '60s and '70s and '80s are playing concerts where they recreate their classic recordings note-for-note. He said those artists made "perfect records" of which the public remembers

Rhythm is the first and most immediately seductive element in music.

the sound very clearly, while he wrote songs and recorded them quickly and imperfectly, and his fans remember the words and maybe the melodies, but the sound of the recordings isn't and wasn't the point. I don't know whether that's absolutely true. "Like a Rolling Stone" has a *very* particular sound that you recognize the second you hear that organ and drum combo, but overall he's correct.

In the "modern" era — for my purposes that would be somewhere after just after Elvis Presley's arrival — the line between songwriting and production has become progressively blurred to the point where producers of pop music now *are* the songwriters. The beats and layering that the producers create in the studio are the primary basis for the song, and the vocal and lyric are merely a part of the sonic spectrum. You know which songwriter has delivered the third most No. 1 songs, after Lennon and McCartney? Swedish producer Max Martin. His 20 smash hits include songs for Britney Spears, NSYNC, Katy Perry, Kelly Clarkson, Pink, Maroon 5 and Taylor Swift — and the artists' involvement in the writing process is unclear.

This comes back to the idea that rhythm is the first and most immediately seductive element in music.

I have to make myself remember that point, especially when I'm recording, so I try to infuse a nice beat into the song. Paul Simon's output is a perfect example of this. He started out very spare: acoustic guitar and two voices, very pretty and lyric/melody/harmony focused. But Simon and Garfunkel couldn't get any real attention until a producer put drums and bass onto "The Sound of Silence," which initially was recorded as a guitar/vocal folk song (for Simon & Garfunkel's debut album, *Wednesday Morning, 3 AM*). Then people loved it. Simon was said to have hated the electric version at first, by the way.

As Simon's career waned in the '80s, he chose to make his most rhythmically infused album, *Graceland*, with African musicians, and it was a big "comeback" record for him. His songs since then have been rhythmically based with mostly simple chords and melodic patterns. His lyric writing has continued to grow and change — and become more poetic and less of a straight narrative. He's a very interesting songwriter, and his work could be used to illustrate a lot of the points we've been discussing here.

For the Beatles it's important not to overlook the musicality and groove of Ringo, who often gets shortchanged when people discuss how those records sound. Have you ever listened to the guitar/vocal demos of some Beatles' songs? They can be pretty dreary. So just getting the songs into the rock band format with Ringo on the kit made a huge difference.

I think for me the song will dictate whether it's gonna be slow, fast or mid-tempo and whether the drumming will be aggressive or gentle or somewhere in between. As a song appears, it usually has an intrinsic feel and suggested mood that I try to stick with. In some cases over the years, I've tried to make songs that appeared as slow/mellow songs turn into rock band songs. In most cases that is a disaster. An example of one that actually benefited from playing around with rhythm is the song "Sweet Is the Anchor." That went through so many ridiculous changes of tempo, form, chords, loud, soft...oh, my. I wish I had some recordings of its various forms. Maybe it's best I don't, actually. But at some point, I landed on the feel that's on the recorded album version, something jaunty and lilting akin to Belle & Sebastian's "The State I Am In," and it just felt right.

Most of the time, though, the initial feel is the right one, and although it's fun to try other approaches, you end up coming back to where it started. I would *like* to write more upbeat, fun, rockin' groove songs, but, as we've said before, when you try to force stuff to happen, it's not usually very good. It has to come naturally. And for me, apparently, mid tempos are where I live.

Here's something along those lines: When Pandora first appeared, I looked at the Dolly Varden stuff up there, and it was classified as "major key" music. I found that very interesting because it had never really occurred to me that almost all my songs are in major keys, as opposed to minor keys. Since then I've pushed myself to write in minor keys more often, but it also made me more aware of how predominant minor keys are in current popular music — hip hop, dance music and pop, whether we're talking about Kanye West, Lady Gaga or Adele.

I think minor keys with a dance or hip hop production sound more "intense" and tough. Interesting, no?

M Pandora classifies music by whether it's in major or minor keys? Learn something new every day. I also never thought of Dolly Varden as being specifically major-key music — or of hip hop and pop being predominantly minor-key music, though I guess Kanye West or Eminem usually is rapping over sinister-sounding minor chords. Minor keys just carry more tension, no? If you want sweet resolution, you go to the major.

But let's table those distinctions for a bit because I don't want to shut the door on the rhythm discussion. Rhythm may involve beats and drums, but of course it can be driven by other elements. McCartney's acoustic guitar playing on "Yesterday," accompanied only by a string quartet, is rhythmic. Words obviously are rhythmic. Rapping often requires no accompaniment, and Dylan — through his peppery rhyming schemes and idiosyncratic way not just with words but syllables — pretty much revolutionized the delivery of folk and rock lyrics regardless of whether he recorded "perfect" versions. I really appreciate how Dylan keeps his songs unpredictable in concert by constantly messing with the arrangements. These are not museum pieces, he's saying; these are living, breathing organisms. They're *alive*. At the same time, though, the "name that song" game he plays with concertgoers can get a bit perverse. He doesn't just change the instrumentation; he also sometimes runs roughshod over the way those precisely written, carefully assembled words *sound*. It's as if he's asking the audience, "OK, how much of 'Positively 4th Street' is left if I sing it with a mouthful of marbles and completely alter the cadences?" If rhythm weren't inherent to those songs, we wouldn't be so confounded when he upends it.

Paul Simon is an interesting case because he so dramatically altered the way he writes, moving from a traditional words-music approach to one in which musicians create a sound bed onto which he constructs the remainder of the song. Yet even in his early days, he showed a keener-than-average interest in rhythm, such as on the bongos-driven "Patterns" from *Parsley, Sage, Rosemary and Thyme* (1966) and the joyful syncopations of "Cecilia" from *Bridge Over Troubled Water* (1970). Simon isn't imposing these rhythms onto the songs; they're intrinsic to the songwriting.

Max Martin, who delivered those smashes for Katy Perry, Taylor Swift and many others, is an instructive example because the modern way of creating hit songs starts with the beats before other elements are layered on in assembly-line fashion. John Seabrook spells out the process in his fascinating 2015 book *The Song Machine*, which contrasts this "track-and-hook" songwriting approach to the "melody-and-lyrics" approach of the Brill Building and Tin Pan Alley eras. With track-and-hook, the producer lays down the initial rhythm track, and different parts of the song — hooks, lyrics, verses, bridges, melodies, even the "vibe" — are farmed out to various specialists. The same track may be sent to multiple people who have the same job — such as "topliners," who come up with primary melodies and lyrics — and the strongest contributions are kept, the rest discarded. No wonder Perry's "California Gurls" boasts six co-writers, including Martin, fellow super-producer Dr. Luke and the artist herself.

The number of collaborators aside, you still might view the current spate of producer/songwriter-driven hits as a throwback to Phil Spector's heyday, when he was writing the songs, hiring the musicians, sculpting the sound and thrusting groups such as the Ronettes and the Crystals into the spotlight. But given that most of us aren't working with committees to create our songs, let's ask this:

How much of songwriting actually involves arranging or what we commonly call producing?

It was the Beatles (again!), with producer George Martin, who popularized the notion that arranging is a key part of the songwriting process. Their recordings are "perfect" because it's usually tough to imagine the songs being presented in a superior form.

Consider "Come Together": It's a Lennon song, infused with his deft, evocative wordplay and sung with characteristic vigor, yet if not for McCartney's slinky bass line and swampy keyboard playing and those fantastic Ringo drum rolls (you're right about him), would it still be the "Come Together" we all know and love? I'd say no. Does that mean that when you sit down to write a song, you must be able to piece together all such elements at that time? Of course not. But it does suggest that working with intuitive, damn fine musicians can make you look like a much better songwriter.

S   As far as the difference between what a song is and what production and arranging are, I tend to favor the old idea that a song should be able to stand up and make an impact with just a single voice and a single piano or guitar. Everything else is production and arranging.

The song is the lyrics, chords, melody and the rhythmic interplay among those elements. The production and arranging are the elements added to make a recording. I know this is quickly becoming an antiquated way of looking at things in the world of modern pop music where the production *is* the song, but I'm sticking with it.

So, in the case of "Come Together" that you mentioned, the song is the words, melody and chords that John Lennon brought in as raw material. Ringo's cool drum part and the signature bass line that Paul added are not intrinsically parts of the song, in my opinion. They are crucial parts of the recording, but the song itself could be strummed on an acoustic guitar and sung, and you'd recognize it immediately.

I would disagree with your assessment that George Martin's contributions to the Beatles recordings are part of the songwriting process. The songs were written prior to his contributions, in most cases. He took the raw materials and discussed and offered options for the recordings.

Let's look at "A Day In The Life." Essentially it is two songs melded together. The bulk of the song is John's beautiful ballad with the gorgeous, melancholy melody and chords. That stands up on its own without anything more than his voice and acoustic guitar. Ringo's orchestral, emotional drumming and the thick, block piano chords certainly bolster the mood and sound cool, but they are not intrinsic to the raw impact of the song itself. The middle section is a rather slight McCartney ditty that was probably an unfinished fragment that, when connected to John's song, adds insight and depth. Whose idea was it to combine the two songs? I'm guessing it was John and Paul's idea. In that case I call it songwriting.

instances. The amazing, rising string section? Arranging and production, in my opinion — not part of the song itself. I look forward to your letters.

In most songs, though, it is not that hard to separate the song from the production. Take away the drums, vocal harmonies, strings, guitar solos, horns, electric sitars, etc., and you still have the singer singing words and melody over chords.

M   Very nicely put, and I agree with your basic point: The song is the song, and it should hold up no matter how spare the arrangement — or how rudimentary the playing behind it is, for that matter. And I don't think George Martin should be getting a songwriting credit on those Beatles classics, but there's no question he made a lot of their songs better. "Please Please Me" initially was Lennon's attempt to write a Roy Orbison-style ballad until Martin got the band to speed it up, as mentioned earlier, and it became their breakthrough hit. Lennon's "Strawberry Fields Forever" was a beautiful song before Martin worked his wonders in knitting together two separate versions originally recorded in different keys and tempos — but the producer did not hold what would become Lennon's subsequent psychedelic effort "I Am the Walrus" in such high esteem. Now I consider "I Am the Walrus" to be a pinnacle of the psychedelic era, but is that because it's such an inherently great song — one that would be just as effective if recorded solo acoustic — or because the swirling strings and layered vocals lift it to a sublime place?

I agree, that's production — and I do love Lennon's wordplay and that insistent music even without the overdubs, so maybe it's a great song after all — but we should all have such intuitive, innovative producers to make our songwriting shine so brightly. Having band-mates as talented as the Beatles also wouldn't hurt.

Now back to the major/minor discussion: You know, if Pandora is going to have a major-key classification, it could employ a whole bunch of other categories. How about one for diatonic songs — that is, those that stick to a single key without ever straying to an outside-the-box chord? You once pointed out that almost all of the Eagles' hits are diatonic. Beatles songs, in contrast, often shift between chords in major and minor keys and may jump to a different key for the middle eight. Different songs play by different rules. Some use parallel-minor chords. Some use relative-minor chords. Some modulate. Some throw down cycles of 4ths or 5ths.

Stop.

Before we get into all this technical stuff, let's back up and address some basic questions:

How much music theory do you need to know to write songs?

How much *should* you know? Is it important to be conscious of what your root key is and whether the natural III or VI chords are major or minor or whether your *song* is major or minor? If you move from one chord to another and you like how that sounds, does anything else matter? If songwriting is ultimately a mysterious, inspiration-driven process, how essential is **knowledge**?

s   Ah, I think we've arrived at something very important and complicated. There is a sort of distrust of music theory knowledge in the rock world. In some ways I share that distrust — but I think for different reasons. I think there's a feeling that rock music is less "pure" if someone has studied music theory. There's also a sort of romantic popular view that I've heard many times that goes, "Paul McCartney/John Lennon/Paul Simon (insert favorite pop/rock icon here) can't read a note of music." That's true in most cases, but it misses the point.

Folk, rock and pop come from the oral tradition that we've talked about here, where the music is passed down through recordings and concerts and learned "by ear." So McCartney may not be able to tell you that the bridge to "Here, There and Everywhere" goes to the parallel minor, but he knows what it sounds like, and he chose that sound purposefully. He could call the key change "Uncle Fred" if he wanted; it wouldn't matter. Only the end result does. Same with John Lennon. There are tons of fancy chord changes on those early Beatles songs, and my guess is they said, "Let's use that chord from that Roy Orbison song or that Ronettes song or the 'Peggy Sue' chord."

There's a funny interview with Paul Simon in which he attempts to tell the theory behind how he got to the bridge chords for a song, but his music theory is almost entirely wrong. Yet it doesn't matter. The chords are still beautifully composed and take the song into a new harmonic area. He chose them for how they sound and the emotional impact of the harmonic movement — and most likely for the melodic opportunities the new chords presented.

Most pop/rock/folk/blues writers follow their ears and their instincts and have a well of reference points from which to pull. Listening to thousands of recordings and learning how to play an instrument have trained their ears and their instincts. It's unfair to the Eagles, or anyone, to criticize their songs for being diatonic (not that you were criticizing). Diatonic chords are great. They sound wonderful, and there are thousands of beloved songs that stay squarely in one key. Complicated harmony doesn't make a song great. It can. But it has to come from a musical place, not an intellectual place. That's what I think, anyway.

Here's the trap for people who begin to learn music theory: Suddenly they are presented with a set of "rules." When they were innocently playing guitar and wandering from D to G to A and singing things that felt right, all was good. But suddenly they are told that that's a I-IV-V progression and that it's been done a billion times before. So the reaction is to try and write complicated, multi-key chord progressions because that must be better, right?

Well, complicated for the sake of being complicated is never better — not with chords, melody or rhythm. In my classes I try to make it clear that there's nothing intrinsically inferior about three- and four-chord songs. Key changes and chords drawn from outside the tonic should happen because of the way they reinforce the mood of the song, not because they are theoretically awesome.

I learned a lot of music theory because I wanted to be a jazz guitarist when I was in high school. It seems crazy now, but I was in love with records by Kenny Burrell, Wes Montgomery, Jim Hall and others. I was also writing songs at the time, so I had a mixed personality in a way: learning jazz guitar and trying to write songs like Neil Young and Paul Simon. I had a great jazz guitar teacher in Idaho who was influential in my desire to learn jazz, who showed me lots of chord voicings and started me with understanding scales and keys. From the beginning I was much better at — and much more interested in — learning chords and voicings and how they fit together.

I went to Berklee and continued studying jazz but moved into jazz composition as my interest in and ability to play jazz on the guitar waned. I also began to realize that my real love was writing and singing songs. But while I was coming to that understanding, I took all the levels of Harmony and found it fascinating. And, yes, the songs I was writing at the time were ridiculously complicated and probably unlistenable. One thing I realized at the highest levels of Harmony is that anything can be anything and that the rules don't really apply. The rules come after the fact and are an attempt to qualify and explain things. Any chord can follow any chord, and you can make a theoretical case for it. So that's total freedom in a way. Full circle. It's like chaos theory!

So I have a ton of knowledge that is there if I need it or want it. I have learned to turn it off when I'm writing unless I have a moment where a certain sound is needed: I know what the diatonic chords will sound like, I know what the secondary dominants will sound like, etc. I still *love* the feeling of wandering from D to G to A, and even if a tiny part of me feels like that's kind of cheap, I still go with it. "California Zephyr," one of my best-loved songs, is G to F to C over and over and over. Do I feel a little bit ashamed of that? Yeah. But, in a way I'm also proud that I made a nice song that people like out of three chords and a bunch of images.

Joni Mitchell used to purposefully put her guitar into unknown tunings so that she could maintain a childlike feeling of discovery as she wrote. That's one way of finding freedom from knowledge. Playing an instrument you don't really "play" is another. But Joni also had written lots of songs in standard tuning before that and had probably learned dozens of folk songs by others, too, so she had accumulated a storehouse of musical knowledge to draw from. Her instincts were stellar.

OK, so if your goal is to write songs from your heart that fit somewhere into the rock/pop world, the best method would be to learn to play a bunch of songs by artists you love and try to absorb what you love about them. Next try to copy them, and ultimately incorporate those things into your own songs, no music theory training needed. You'll learn how the chords sound together by ear. That would be the way most, if not all, of the people we've been discussing did it. If your goal is to write songs for Broadway or in the jazz world, you're going to want to study music theory so you can communicate within those worlds and so you can understand the structures of the songs. If you want to be an instrumentalist who can play in a variety of styles and situations, it is imperative that you understand music theory, I think.

M I wrestle with this question all the time, regarding not only what I know but also what I can play — which is to say I'm not exactly versatile when it comes to musicianship. I think your advice about learning songs that you love is sound. My introduction to songwriting came as sort of an offshoot to my obsessive listening to Simon & Garfunkel, the Beatles and their solo offshoots, E.L.O., Billy Joel (yes, Billy Joel, at least for a bit), Supertramp (I thought Supertramp was an Important Band when I was much younger, and that was my first concert ever), Steely Dan and Pink Floyd — and then my transition into the post-punk world of Elvis Costello, Talking Heads, XTC, Squeeze, R.E.M. and the Feelies. My M.O. was to get hooked on one album and then to go back and absorb the entire catalog: Hey, this Procol Harum album *A Salty Dog* sure is cool — time to hit the used-record stores and find *Shine on Brightly* and everything else.

These songs would provide me a constant mental soundtrack all day long. No matter what I was doing, a significant portion of brain space was (and is) devoted to music. When I was in high school, a snatch of melody occasionally would pop into my head that wasn't from one of those records, and I would replay it over and over. Where did it come from? Did I just make it up? Was I subconsciously stealing it from some existing song? I'd walk down the school hallways toying with the tune in my head and trying to add to it. A chorus would beget verses, or vice versa. A vocal line would emerge, maybe some words as well. I'd hear a piano phrase or maybe a guitar riff. And I couldn't play any of it.

I took piano when I was in elementary school and had a teacher, a fairly old woman, who yelled at me when I screwed up, which was all too frequent. She also wouldn't assign me any songs that I knew aside from, in her one gesture of largesse, the *Fiddler on the Roof* soundtrack. I didn't practice enough. I let it go and always regretted it. In junior high I took guitar lessons from a very nice guy who taught out of his basement. He would record *Monty Python* episodes on his reel-to-reel tape recorder (in those pre-VCR days) and play back sketches during our lessons. They were hilarious. He also had me play parody versions of songs such as Cat Stevens' "Moon Shadow" ("I'm being followed by a big monster…"). We laughed a lot, but I didn't learn much guitar. Again, the main culprit was my own lack of discipline in practicing.

Toward the end of college, I realized I wanted to be able to play guitar after all. I bought a cheap Japanese Stratocaster knock-off and an old, used Ampeg tube amp that had just one effect: tremolo. I loved tremolo. I'd play the "Crimson and Clover" riff over and over and over. A few years later I bought an acoustic guitar as well, and that's been my primary instrument ever since. And guess what? I still don't practice enough, and I'm not much of a player, though I pretty much can communicate a song.

Soon after I picked up that electric guitar and strummed the various chords that I knew, songs began suggesting themselves. The first was an upbeat ditty called "Looking for an Hour" that alternated between G to C before jumping to Em, A, Am and then back to C. The next one, concocted under the influence of *Big Star's 3*rd as I recall, was slow and awash in my beloved tremolo as the verse repeated an A7-E-D-A progression before landing on a C instead of A to ease the transition to a chorus that went G-C-G-G-C-Am-F-Em. I still couldn't tell you how these chords relate to the tonic or even what the base key is, though the song feels like it wants to wind up on G. I had taken a music-theory class in college and can read music in a rudimentary notes-recognizing sort of way, but the writing process — which would be more accurately described as the making-up process — was wholly instinctual.

Yet knowledge, what little I had, helped. Sometime a friend would teach me a new chord, and I would make it the basis of a song. Sometimes I'd stick the capo on the third or the fifth fret, and that difference in tone would point me down a new path. Still, I had almost no real clue of what I was doing. I suspect in my random explorations of chords, I was landing on combinations that I'd heard in Beatles, R.E.M., Feelies, XTC or Big Star songs (though not Steely Dan songs — I never could play those chords, though in my head I have written the previously nonexistent title track to *Can't Buy a Thrill*).

My so-called writing remains a combination of the mental (a song fragment comes to me while I'm doing something else) and physical (I make a discovery on the guitar or piano that gets me going). My sense is if you keep using the same songwriting methods and tools over the years, you may wind up spinning your wheels; all too many careers bear out the difficulty of remaining fresh and vibrant long-term. So I'd think the more you can keep adding to your knowledge base, the less likely it is that your ideas well will dry up. One of your class assignments that I especially enjoyed directed us to construct melodies solely from notes in the pentatonic scale. That forced me to write on the piano (I couldn't have identified all of those notes on a guitar) and led to a pretty, sad melody that I never would have found without those limitations. I was pleased to discover that the underlying chords were suitably weird as well.

In contrast, the first song I wrote for your class, "Kicking It Out," was composed mostly in my head, and I was disappointed when I pulled out my guitar to discover that I'd come up with a shopworn I-IV-V progression (albeit with an unexpected jump for the bridge). But that doesn't matter, right? It's still a catchy tune.

I like to think of myself as a melody guy, both in what I listen to and what I come up with. Yet I find the process of creating melodies to be completely mysterious. As I said before, I've often wondered whether I wasn't just ripping off something I'd previously heard — or creating something that someone somewhere had created before. At

times I *have* discovered the roots of my hooks or melody snatches in
other songs, but I'm happy to say those have been the exceptions rather
than the rule.

Still, there's a finite number of melodies, chord changes and
combinations out there, no? Blues songs recycle the same progressions
ad infinitum, and no one blinks. In the rock-pop world, there's a bit
more emphasis on newness, though by this point you could find an
uncanny mash-up partner for almost any song. So…

How do you know that what you're creating is yours?

And for a relative babe in the songwriting woods, what would
you have that person learn first?

s   Very interesting. You being a "melody guy," which I think is
accurate, is a great thing to be but probably the hardest to
make work without a working knowledge of how the notes
you're hearing translate into chords — *or* a tremendous amount
of time to dedicate to the trial-and-error work of finding chords
that accommodate the melody you're hearing. So that's where
a bit of theory knowledge could come in handy.

Say you're singing a melody that goes B G A B D E D. Within
that melody there are a few chords suggested, and you, as composer,
can choose how to color it. A G major chord would work over the whole
thing (G major = G, B and D). An E minor would also work, and would
paint a more melancholy mood. (E minor = E G B). You could get wacky
and play a Cmajor7, and then your melody notes would be "color" tones
primarily. Then you *might* start sounding like those Steely Dan records!

Without knowing what notes you're hearing and what chords
can accommodate those notes, you have a lot more work to do hunt-
ing around for chords. I think people who play piano have an easier
time doing this sort of thing; they can see the notes they're playing and
see combinations of chords that include those notes. I don't think it's
a coincidence that most great melody songwriters are primarily piano
players: Brian Wilson, Burt Bacharach, Richard Rogers. Paul McCartney
would be the exception; though he's a fine piano player, some of his best
melodies were written to a guitar backing. He's a special case, though,
in a lot of ways. Guitar is very illogical in its layout. It takes a long time to
make the connection of what notes you're actually playing and where
they are on the instrument.

In regards to your question, I think the idea of writing what's "yours" is an incorrect way to see things. That's a big fear among beginning songwriters, and it often stops them in their tracks. The truth is we all start by copying, and that's a good thing, for the reasons discussed above about how to learn what you like and don't like. No one starts out completely original. You learn songs by copying others and then slowly begin to pick and choose the stuff you like and don't like, creating your own personal amalgam of musical choices.

No two human voices are alike, and everyone has a slightly different feel for rhythms, so you can't help but sound like yourself unless you're consciously trying to impersonate someone — like if you were the John Lennon in a Beatles cover band — but even then it doesn't really

I'd say worry less about being original and more about being truthful.

sound exactly like Lennon, right? I tell people not to worry so much about being original, that it will happen naturally if they stay true to themselves and try not to make adjustments based on what they think people will like (or not like) or what they think they're supposed to do. Even Captain Beefheart probably started out singing "normal" songs and learning blues songs, etc., and then trusted his own weird sense of language and timing enough to go off into his own thing.

A good songwriting exercise for new writers, or anyone actually, is to write new words to an existing song, matching the syllable count, rhyme scheme, etc. When you do something like this you'll begin to really respect Weird Al — if you don't already! Then, if you like the new lyric, you can write new music to it and have a brand new, all-original song. You can also lift chord changes from an existing song and change the order of one or two and, *presto*, new song.

I'd say worry less about being original and more about being truthful.

M First, to continue my Beatles fixation, it would be interesting to see a breakdown of McCartney's greatest melodies written on piano/keyboard vs. guitar. Though I really don't know how he wrote all of these, the prominence of keyboards would suggest the piano/keyboard category might include "Hey Jude,"

"Let It Be," "Good Day Sunshine," "For No One," "Penny Lane," his Mellotron intro to "Strawberry Fields Forever," the middle part of "A Day in the Life," "The Fool on the Hill," "Lady Madonna," "The Long and Winding Road," You Never Give Me Your Money," "Golden Slumbers," "Maybe I'm Amazed" and "My Love," among others. Not bad. He has said he dreamed up the melody to "Yesterday" (as "Scrambled Eggs"), so the guitar doesn't get credit there. I'm thinking the guitar list would include "All My Loving," "And I Love Her," "Things We Said Today," "I'll Follow the Sun," "Here, There and Everywhere," "Blackbird," "I Will," "Mother Nature's Son" and many of his rockers. Bottom line: Dude has a gift for melodies regardless of the instrument.

Quick aside: You ever notice that apart from "Tomorrow Never Knows," all of John's songs on *Revolver* are driven by electric guitar and none of Paul's are? ("Paperback Writer," a concurrent single, would be the exception.)

As for me, I don't want to put myself in the anti-knowledge camp, but I will say I haven't found matching chords to melodies to be too much work. When I'm composing while I'm playing, the chords suggest the melodies, and when I come up with melodies first, they usually suggest the chords, which don't take *too* long to find on the guitar or piano, perhaps because I don't know that many chords. Then again, I do get vexed when I can't find the chord in my head and suspect it's one I don't know how to play. I have no idea how idiosyncratic my approach is — everyone's songwriting methods are probably idiosyncratic in their own ways — but it's not a conscious process. I'm not aware of what notes I'm singing or what the notes of the corresponding chords are, though you're right in that when I've written on the piano, I do see the melody notes on my right hand and can match them more easily to chords on my left. But in most cases, I'm creating by feel, "hearing" what the chord should sound like and then trying to translate that into what I play.

That said, I know I'm missing out on shadings, variations and possibilities. Perhaps I could find better or more interesting chords than what I'm "hearing." Maybe if I could play more chords and notes up and down the guitar neck, I would add depth, complexity, texture. Given that learning new chords sometimes has served as a jumping-off point for writing new songs, I certainly should obtain a better working knowledge of diminished chords, 6ths and other less rudimentary configurations.

I always acknowledge that I *should* play better and more often, but my rationalization has been that when I finally record my master-piece around the time that Social Security kicks in, I'll make sure to work with someone more skilled than I who can help me color inside the lines. Then again, I've played songs for some expert musicians, and occasionally they have told me why I should play a different chord than I'm playing. They have a strong musical foundation for what they're saying, and sometimes I think, Hmm, I ought to try that, but in other cases I know they're wrong because *that's not how the song goes.* You know why this chord is right? *Because I said so.*

Part of being a songwriter is developing a stubborn-artist streak, right? On the originality front, it seems like there are two extremes: One would be to come into songwriting with absolutely no foundation of anything, like you've never even heard music so there could be zero influences on your work; and the other would be to bring so many influences to the table that there's no way to unscramble them, and thus your way of combining them is inherently unique to you. I lean toward the latter group.

As I said before, I've always been an obsessive listener, and those particular obsessions are my own, as is my way of processing them. So when I write, this vast mental encyclopedia of music no doubt is informing every note, but I'd be hard put to deconstruct how — and if I did, I'd probably be wrong. I tried writing a country song recently, but my idea of country is far removed from commercial Nashville or rootsy Austin, and when I've played it for friends, they've said, "That's not a country song." But they liked it enough as a song-song, so I'm OK with that, even if I have no idea where my notion of "country" comes from. I remember reading years ago that Camper Van Beethoven approached "Eye of Fatima" as their Creedence Clearwater Revival song, and I thought: Wha'? But, hey, if such a cool tune results from Camper attempting to channel Creedence, they should do that sort of thing more often. The Hollies' excellent, uncharacteristic "Long Cool Woman (in a Black Dress)" sounds like they were trying to channel Creedence as well; maybe everyone should try that.

Bottom line: So much in the air is influencing all of us that there's no way to break it all down.

So, yes, I agree that one shouldn't let the quest for originality inhibit the creative process. At the same time, though, sometimes you find that what you've created is awfully similar to something that has preceded it. I remember in one of your classes someone presented a song revolving around the phrase "Love is the drug I'm thinking of," and we all agreed it was a little too close for comfort to the Roxy Music single. George Harrison learned this lesson the hard way when a U.S. district court found that he had "subconsciously" plagiarized the Chiffons' "He's So Fine" with "My Sweet Lord." Ray Parker, Jr. also had to settle a suit over the similarity of his "Ghostbusters" to Huey Lewis and the News' "I Want a New Drug," Sam Smith is sharing royalties with Tom Petty and Jeff Lynne thanks to the echoes of "I Won't Back Down" in "Stay with Me," and a jury ordered Robin Thicke and Pharrell Williams to pay $7.4 million to Marvin Gaye's family as compensation for Thicke's "Blurred Lines" infringing upon the copyright of Gaye's "Got To Give it Up," though for that last one I always heard more of a similarity in the arrangements than the melodies. My friends and I used to make a sport of finding parts of songs seemingly nicked from other songs.

But then I have discovered echoes of my own hooks in earlier songs, such as one that somehow mixes in bits of the Steve Miller Band's "Jungle Love" and Peter Frampton's "Do You Feel Like We Do" (!) or another with a bridge similar to that of Sam Phillips' "Holding on to the Earth" or one that seemingly transfers the organ riff of Elvis Costello and the Attractions' "This Year's Girl" to a guitar, albeit with a slightly different rhythm. I feel like I should make adjustments because the similarities bother me, but then again, that's how these songs go. Are these actionable offenses or just the reality of pop-rock songwriting? I have one song with a percussion opening just like that of the White Stripes' "My Doorbell," but I made my home cassette a good decade earlier, and I guarantee that Jack White never heard it.

Have you ever changed a song upon finding something similar in a previously recorded piece?

And, to get down to the nitty-gritty:

What are five things any fledgling songwriter should know?

Ready? Go.

S   I threw away a song once because I realized the chord sequence and a few melody notes were exactly from a U2 song. I can't remember which one. I tried re-arranging the chords and melody, but in the end I didn't find the song engaging enough to fight for it. I've had people point out similarities between my songs and some famous songs before, usually not enough to worry about.

One time, though, someone pointed out that the chords and melody to the verses of Dolly Varden's "Complete Resistance" are a rip-off of the Rolling Stones' "Wild Horses," and, you know what? They are. I teach "Wild Horses" in guitar classes all the time and know the song inside out, but it was completely an unconscious rip-off. I really had *no* idea. This must be what happened with George Harrison and "My Sweet Lord." In that case, though, you'd think Phil Spector would have recognized the similarity and asked George to change the melody a little. In my case the song was out and released before I could change it. Now I kind of hate that song. I consider it a misfire. It's a bummer that we opened the record with it! There's a situation where an outside producer could have come in handy. Oh, well!

OK, I've thought a lot about this list of 5 things. Most are based on things students say on a regular basis in songwriting class.

1. You will end up writing some sad songs, even if you are a "happy" person. It is very difficult to write an actual "happy" song. It's hard to write about happiness without falling into clichés or generalizations about sunshine or flying, etc. Even songs that we consider "happy" often are imbued with memories of hardship or are aware impending sadness. I remember once saying to someone how "Wouldn't It Be Nice" was the happiest song ever, and he said, "That song is the saddest song in the world. It's about the realization that the scenario painted is an impossible fantasy he will never attain." Yipes. But kinda true!

Songs are also a culturally acceptable place to share feelings and thoughts of hardship and sadness. Shared experience, common ground. Everyone experiences hardships, heartbreaks, mortality — songs give voice to these things, as well as happy times like in "Good Day Sunshine," etc. This relates back to the "listening" vs. "celebration" duality of songs.

Side note: Have you noticed how many upbeat, fun-sounding songs are super bleak lyrically? I was just going through "(Don't Go Back to) Rockville" with someone. Bleak and cranky lyrics to a jangly, happy-go-lucky tune.

Side note 2: I personally *hate* the word "depressing" as a descriptor of songs, as in "Oh, Nick Drake's songs are so depressing!" Exploring sadness is very different from being depressing, I think. Listening to Nick Drake or Elliot Smith, I'm moved by the chords and melodies and the artfulness of the lyrics; the songs at their best transcend the utter sadness of the words and create something beautiful. Thinking about their tragic lives is depressing. There's a difference there, right?

I've had people get upset when they keep writing "sad" songs, as if there must be something wrong with them. I've also noticed that just being thoughtful and sensitive to the world around us comes across as "sad" to these people. It freaks them out that they aren't writing, "I'm walking on sunshine" all the time. I tell them to keep writing, and they'll eventually get to a happy song or two. That leads me to...

2. Songs tend to dictate their own direction. You usually can't control where a song wants to go — and you shouldn't try. You might start out thinking you're writing a song about your 7th grade crush, but you might end up in the Spanish Civil War. If you try too hard to stay with the 7th grade crush, you'll deny the song (and your imagination) the joy of the exploration. That usually leads to a song that has a verse and a half and nowhere to go. Let 'em go where they wanna go. It's hard to let go.

3. Finish your "bad" songs. You'll probably learn more finishing off the crappy songs than you will writing your masterpiece. The good ones tend to come out pretty solid. The bad ones really need a lot of crafting and work. Writing the third verse to a terrible song is a great exercise. You don't have to sing it for anyone, but do the work.

4. The only way to really learn how to write songs is to write songs. Some people get lucky, and their first songs are quite good, but the rest of us have to write dozens of awful songs as we figure out what works and what doesn't. Don't be discouraged that your songs are filled with forced rhymes, boring chords, trite metaphors, two-note melodies, and they sound like music you don't like. It'll get better. Don't give up!

5. If you want to write songs, you need to designate a quiet space where you won't be interrupted, where your cell phone is either off or in another room and the Internet is off. You need to make an agreement with the people you live with that they won't bug you. You need to feel that you can make mistakes and no one will judge you — so that means no one can hear you. If you think someone is listening in, your self-critical voice will have power over you, and you'll probably never get to the good stuff.

Bonus thought: If you're looking to get rich from writing songs, you'd be better off playing the lottery. If you approach songwriting as "product," your songs will sound like "product." Of course, there are going to be exceptions. Occasionally the song-by-committee hit writers in Nashville or L.A. churn out a good one that people will be singing years from now, but that's rare. Most of the hit songs written to be hit songs sound generic and lifeless just months after they are hits. Because they are. Well crafted? Yes. Inspired, true and unique? No.

The world is already filled with enough crappy made-for-market songs. Aim higher. The songs that last are the ones that come from the heart. A cliché, yes, but true. Follow your heart, and don't think about writing hits. That's not to say you shouldn't pursue, explore and be open to each and every opportunity that your songs can find. You should sing your best songs for anyone who'll listen, and if you make money from them, fantastic. Win win!

M As you know I'm fascinated by the phenomenon of the hit record, and I think you've touched upon one of the great fallacies about creating one. People think: I should write a song like *that* one. And certainly there's no shortage of copycat hits. But the songs that really stand out, the ones that leave their mark and last, are those that occupy their own unique spaces. This makes sense: The reason your ears perk up when you hear that undeniable hit is that it sounds **different**.

Extreme example: "Bohemian Rhapsody." Another Queen one, this time with David Bowie: "Under Pressure." What an utterly weird song, structure-wise and otherwise; nothing sounds remotely like it, except maybe "Ice Ice Baby" (speaking of rip-offs…). The retro yet modern bass groove of Gnarls Barkley's "Crazy" popped out of the speakers like no other songs being played on the radio at that time. Amy Winehouse's "Rehab" and "You Know I'm No Good" are personal

The reason your ears perk up when you hear that undeniable hit is that it sounds *different*.

— tragically so in retrospect — yet also undeniably catchy in an updated soul-sister kind of way that became much copied. Adele's *21* is packed with intimate broken-hearted songs presented without the kind of studio manipulations that drive much of contemporary hit radio, and "Rolling in the Deep" was a real powerhouse. No album that year came close to it sales-wise or acclaim-wise. When "Hello" introduced her album *25* at the end of 2015, you heard those stately piano chords and may have thought: Well, that sounds familiar. Much of the album did. But then that "Hello" chorus…undeniable. There are worse messages that the music industry could deliver than be like Adele.

I'm with you on your "depressing" gripe as well. Depression generally involves a state of feeling alone and isolated, yet Nick Drake, Elliot Smith and Richard Thompson (who called a fan-club cassette compilation *Doom and Gloom from the Tomb*) each offers the listener a kindred spirit, someone who not only shares dark feelings but also infuses them with beauty. I've been lifted out of many a funk by listening to so-called depressing music.

That said, Thompson's "End of the Rainbow," in which he informs a baby, "There's nothing at the end of the rainbow/There's nothing to grow up for anymore," is pretty damn depressing.

So, yes, in agreement with your first point about sad songs and shared experiences, the best route to universality is through specificity. The world is filled with *so many songs* — like jillions and gazillions of them — that there's no shortage of blah-blah generalities about love, pain, anger, etc. Let's say you'd like to sing a song about the rain. Great. Just make sure you have some fresh observations or compelling incidents to offer because there are already too damn many songs about the rain. Cracker even recorded one called "Another Song about the Rain." Adele's approach was to "Set Fire to the Rain," which at least is different.

Of course, striking that personal/universal balance is tricky. I dislike that feeling of listening to a therapy session set to music. Conveying how happy or sad you are or how much pain you're suffering isn't enough. No one wants to hear some stranger wallow. You've got to answer the question, consciously or unconsciously, "Why should anyone care?" The stories you tell, the emotions you convey, must somehow shoot out a thread that pierces the listener's heart.

Your second point about songs dictating their own direction is good advice for almost any kind of writing. It certainly applies to fiction: Rather than trying to control your universe like a master puppeteer, let the characters take you somewhere interesting. And I guess that harks back to the discussion about originality; sometimes a song will veer close to another song, and the writer might have a hard time steering it away by changing a few notes or chords. That said, I'm irritated with whomever told you that "Complete Resistance" is a rip-off of "Wild Horses," because its melodies are quite different, as are the songs' overall feels. (Yours is more Jayhawks-in-Beatles mode than Stonesy.) I'm annoyed that some person has given you reason to turn against what's actually a strong song that found you stretching out sonically. That's wrong. Play it again, Steve!

As for point No. 3, I'd expand it to say: **Finish your songs, period.** I don't leave just bad songs uncompleted; I have some alleged masterpieces languishing in scrap form because I can't get myself to fill in the gaps. Part of that complete resistance (so to speak) may be a fear of gumming up what might be a really good song with lyrics that fall short. And part of it is that old lack of discipline. That's another reason I loved your class: because each session presented a deadline, so I had to finish — and also because when I was writing a song in a week, I didn't have time to overthink and overinvest in it as I might do with a song that's been kicking around for a while. Hey, the germ of this song didn't even exist a few days ago, so why not take chances?

(Subsequent to this exchange, Mark convinced Steve to offer a class called "Finish Your Damn Songs." It was very popular, and Mark finished several damn songs.)

With your fourth point about learning to write songs by writing songs, it's instructive to consider when great songwriters peak. You listen to Lennon and McCartney's pre-Parlophone songs, and there's nothing to indicate that they're about to become rock's — or even popular music's — greatest songwriters. "Love Me Do" was way better than, say, the Decca tryout song "Hello, Little Girl"; "Please Please Me" was way better than "Love Me Do"; "She Loves You" eclipsed "Please Please Me," and they kept topping themselves for years. George Harrison and fellow British Invaders the Rolling Stones (Jagger & Richards), the Kinks (Ray Davies) and the Who (Pete Townshend) took awhile to hit their songwriting strides, as did the Beach Boys (Brian Wilson) and Simon & Garfunkel (Paul Simon).

In general when you think about artists with long careers, their first albums are rarely their best. On the flip side, acts that never top their initial releases tend to have shorter life spans. So, yeah, as you keep writing, it should be getting better all the time — or at least for a while.

Finally, that quiet-space issue is one of my problems, and alibis. We've got no basement, and the kids and wife go to bed early, so finding a good time to play can be challenging. The lesson: Don't wait till you're married with children before you get serious about your music. No, actually, don't blame your wife and kids for your lack of musical commitment; just play and create.

Let's now move on to…

Song structure. How important do you think it is, and how conscious should you be of it?

Should a song "get to the chorus" in a certain amount of time, as the hit-makers in movies like to say?

Does a song need a chorus unless it's a Dylan song?

Do you need to know what part of your song the chorus is? Isn't Pink Floyd's "Another Brick in the Wall, Part 2" essentially just a long chorus repeated a couple times with no verses? Isn't George Harrison's "Give Me Love (Give Me Peace on Earth)" essentially a chorus and a bridge with no actual verses?

When do you need a bridge anyway, and when would it just weigh the song down? How does Tom Petty's "Breakdown" get away with having just one verse, then the chorus, then a guitar solo and then the chorus repeated, and that's it? Why doesn't "California Zephyr" have a bridge, for that matter?

Is this all a matter of that thing called feel?

S   I do think that understanding song form is really important, even if you choose to ignore it when you're writing. It's the ol' "learn the rules so you can break 'em" rule. All of the examples you mentioned above are by songwriters who've also written songs with elaborate structures — myself included!

My guess with "Give Me Love," and probably the others listed, is that George attempted to write other parts, and they didn't work; they probably distracted from rather than enhanced the song. So as someone who had written and/or performed on many, many good records, he used his instincts and decided to go with the basic minimal statement repeated three times with new elements added to the arrangement each time.

With "Zephyr" it never actually occurred to me to write a bridge. That's a weird one; the chorus is wordless over the same chords as the verses. It's basically a three-chord groove with a lyric filled with stuff no one could possibly make full sense of. Why does it work? I don't know. I think it's the overall sound.

We haven't actually talked much about that, but I think that the overall sound of a recording is more important that any of the elements of the song itself, at least with rock and its many subcategories. For me, most of the time, I'm drawn to the sound of the singer's voice, and that's what pulls me in. If I don't like the sound of the voice, it is very difficult to enjoy the song, even if I know I'm "supposed" to like it. I think this is the case for lots of people. Maybe the sound that draws others in is the drums or the guitars or the overall mix of instruments and voices. For some I think it's just the energy and emotion embedded in the sounds on the recording. Certainly a good melody, chord progression and some decent words help! But, honestly, I always ask my classes how many people actually pay attention to the words in songs, and it's usually 20 percent or less.

OK, back to form... I spend an entire class in Songwriting 1 talking about, and playing examples of, various song forms and discussing in detail the basic function of each part. I start with verse form — ballad style — where there's no refrain or chorus of any kind. I use Lucinda Williams' "Pineola," a story song filled with stark, arresting imagery. Then I get to verses with refrains and use Dylan as an example. This is his preferred song form, and he is the master of it. It's a powerful form when the refrain line works and each verse culminates in the end line. I used to use "Tangled up in Blue" as the example, but it's so long. I use "The Times They Are A-Changin'" now; both of those songs land on the title line at the end of each verse. Just the concept of the refrain is usually eye-opening to people. I think even though folks have heard these types of songs lots of times, the concept is still something they hadn't considered. It is freeing to some writers to realize that a full chorus isn't always needed.

In my own writing I often use the verse-with-refrain form; I think it's my natural inclination. I have to work hard to find a chorus. One of the most fascinating things to me is that many Beatles songs don't have full choruses. Quite a lot of their songs follow this form pattern:

Introduction

Verse with refrain

Verse with refrain

Bridge

Verse with refrain

Repeat bridge

Repeat 1st or 3rd verse with refrain

Ending or coda of some sort

Before I started "teaching" songwriting, this hadn't really occurred to me. Here's the big question for Sir Paul next time you talk to him: Is the "We can work it out" part of "We Can Work It Out" a chorus or a refrain? He sings it twice. So is it a very short chorus or a double refrain?

M There seems to be much gray area surrounding these terms, especially when the Beatles are involved. They were clever blokes, no? They also were masters of a song element that isn't generally discussed in terms of structure yet is essential to creating something that sticks in listeners' ears: the hook.

This is kind of a slippery term, because the hook can be something concrete and obvious, like the opening riff of "Start Me Up" or countless Rolling Stones songs or the "Wee-hoo!" of Blur's "Song 2," but it also can be a chord change, a key change, a pithy phrase, a catchy snatch of melody, a more insidious turn of tune, an infectious beat or even a random noise. Queen's "We Will Rock You" hooks you with those first three stomp-and-clap beats. The elevating element of Radiohead's "Creep" is that stuttering guitar scratch that sneaks in just before the chorus. (Meanwhile, the band had to share songwriting credits with the co-writers of the Hollies' "The Air That I Breathe" after a plagiarism suit over the bridge's melody.) And my theory on Bon Jovi's "Livin' on a Prayer" has been that the verses could have been *anything* (the existing ones aren't so distinguished) with no impact on the song thanks to the killer hook in that sing-along chorus, specifically the "Oh-*OH*!" right before "Livin' on a prayer!" That's a hook made for stadium chanting.

Where do these hooks come from? How do you make them happen?

Can you consciously write a hook as you would a chorus or a verse?

S I think you can *try* consciously to write a hook by hammering out short, repeating phrases until something feels both interesting and easy to remember. Short bits of melody, lyrics or rhythm would work best, but a cycle of chord changes could work, too. You also could have a sonic hook created in the recording studio that is interesting and unique. Something like that would go into the grey area between actual songwriting and production, so let's just stick to hooks that are embedded into the songs themselves. Like I said, you can try to contrive a hook, but probably the ideas will sound forced, mechanical and labored over. Here's the hard-truth part: Some people just have a knack for coming up with great hooks. They don't consciously work them out at the piano or guitar; hooks just bubble up naturally as a part of their songwriting process. Those, of course, make the best hooks. As with all aspects of songwriting, the stuff that comes naturally and is uniquely yours is always best and more interesting. The more you *try* to make something happen, the less likely it actually *will* happen. Sad, right?

There are ways to work with this, though, so don't give up, dear readers. In an interview Paul Simon talks about a meeting he had with Paul McCartney sometime in the '80s. He played Sir Paul some tracks he was working on and, as he tells it, McCartney began improvising melodies off the top of his head. Simon said that the stuff McCartney was coming up with was really, really good and seemed to come out of nowhere. As you'd expect, McCartney has a vast, deep well of catchy, beautiful and unique melodic ideas. OK, fine. Where does that leave the rest of us?

Simon is, of course, no slouch when it comes to hooky melodies, but he says he has had to work and work at it. Here's what I would suggest: You can train yourself to become more "hooky" by listening to and absorbing music that is filled with hooks. Listening to and studying Beatles' songs wouldn't be a bad idea. They really understood how to make each song jump out in a unique way and stick with a listener. Guitar parts, lyric phrases, melodic phrases, chord cycles, shouts and other non-lyric vocal sounds (or Lennon's "shoot me" in "Come Together," which sounds more like a sound than a lyric), rhythmic parts (drum breaks, hand claps), instruments not normally found on pop/rock records (sitar, for example) were all explored with great success.

A bit of background: Over the past 100 years or so, popular music has moved from being a primarily melodic art form — say, from the 1920s to the mid 1960s — to its current state of being primarily rhythmic. That's why the hooks in current pop tend to be very short, simple phrases or shouts that are repeated over and over in a rhythmic fashion. The hooks in the big band era were melodic ones. Think of Glenn Miller's "In The Mood," and you'll be singing that phrase in your head all day. The Beatles presided over the transitional period, bridging the two eras. They absorbed the melodic music of their childhoods and were inspired by the more rhythmic early rock 'n' roll of Little Richard, Elvis Presley and Chuck Berry.

for hooks by listening to great hooky music from the past, I think it's important to absorb it more deeply by singing the songs out loud and/or learning to play them. Make a playlist of great, hooky songs and have it on while you're driving around, making dinner or going to sleep. Pick a few great songs that are filled with hooks and learn them inside out, and then try to write songs that feel and sound like that. Keep trying. You can also steal hooks and invert them or restructure them in a way to make them your own. Pop music has always been written by thieves so don't feel guilty borrowing ideas from others. Along the way maybe try to channel your own inner Sir Paul. If you do all that, at some point when you least expect it, you'll come up with a great, hooky song seemingly out of nowhere.

M   It's true that the hookiest hooks I've written have seemed to arrive like lightning strikes — and sometimes as a listener I feel like I can smell overly contrived hooks. (I realize that's a sensory mixed metaphor, but it does feel that way.) As undeniable as Queen's "We Will Rock You" is, the band's later attempt to create another stadium anthem, "I Want It All," arrived like gift-wrapped moldy bread. For years after their hit-making peaks, Prince and the Rolling Stones continued to record songs that sounded like Prince and the Rolling Stones, yet they weren't able to capture more of that proverbial lightning in a bottle; the indelible hook had gone AWOL. Even McCartney, whose melodic facility continues to amaze, hasn't come up with a truly world-conquering hook in decades, though his 2013 album *New* was filled with beautifully crafted pop songs, and the title track was his most delightfully ear-wormy in many years.

I remember hearing the Fitz and the Tantrums song "Out of My League" for the first time; it's got that '80s Hall & Oates feel and an insistent hook that goes "Doo doo doo doo-doo doo-doo-doo." I mean, it's *really* insistent — so insistent that my initial impulse was to think: Dude, back off, you're tugging too hard. I'd liked most of the band's first, more '60s-soul-inspired album, *Pickin' Up the Pieces*, but this just felt like a bald attempt to contrive a sing-along. Months later the song got a lot of airplay, and I guess it must've worn me down a bit because I grew less hostile toward it. That's the funny thing about radio and repetition: You just get used to songs and sounds. Then you hear them too much and get annoyed all over again.

So what's the deal with repetition? Is it a good thing to hammer home the catchy bits over and over, or is it better to leave 'em wanting more?

How much repetition is just right, and when is it too much?

s   That is a tough one and is usually best decided on a case-by-case basis. I remember someone in composition at Berklee talking about the rule of 3's. Sets of 3 are very appealing in music (and other things). Our ears like to hear things once, twice, thrice, but four times is often too many. The basic reason is expectation vs. surprise. If you hear something once, it is new and fresh. If you hear it again and you liked it the first time, that feeling will be reinforced. Hearing it a third time might be pushing it too far, especially if it's not worth repeating, but if it's a good line and/or melody, you might be happy. To go *again* for No. 4 is usually really pushing it. It's my biggest complaint with modern pop: the endless repeats. They drive me crazy. It ends up sounding like music for 2 year olds.

If you can vary it — say give 'em just two times the first time around, then add another repeat the next chorus — then you've got some surprise. Or the opposite: Create the expectation that they'll hear three repeats each chorus, then give them only one or two in a mid-song chorus. Or you can sing the same lyric and melody over a new set of chords that will add some surprise. If it becomes utterly predictable, it's no longer moving. Then it starts to sound silly, to me at least. I recall a teacher at Berklee using Springsteen's "I'm Going Down" as an example of too much repetition. He sings, "I'm going down, down, down, down" so many times it becomes like a joke. Of course, that was a massive hit, so what do they know?

I tend to not repeat stuff as much as I probably should. I find that songwriting students aren't comfortable with repeating stuff, either. But I do feel that I know a good hook when I come across one, and I will repeat it if I feel it's warranted. I come very much out of the Beatles songwriting world, and if you analyze those songs, you'll notice that they don't repeat stuff nearly as much as you think they do. Someone will now bring up the "na na na" part of "Hey Jude" or the ending of "I Want You (She's So Heavy)." Duly noted, thank you. Now listen to most of the rest of their songs.

I think writers should understand what the function of verses, refrains, choruses and bridges are. They are all useful tools and have important, specific functions. A bridge is not a must. A bridge is there to create a new surprise after we've gotten used to the other parts. That's why it is very rare to find a bridge in the first half of a song. A bridge should be a release from the predictability of the song. I find students try to put bridges in after the first chorus or even before the first chorus, which defeats the whole purpose and just makes listening confusing.

Lastly I've been thinking about origins of repetition in songs and why humans are so drawn to hearing and singing a phrase again and again. I'm sure it goes back to pre-historic chanting and drumming and dancing. Call and response. The original meaning of "chorus" comes from the Greek, right? A group standing to the side of the action singing or commenting on the action. I'm trying to make sense of the connection there — how are the Greek chorus and the pop song chorus related?

M   Hmmm. In a classic Greek drama, the chorus is talking directly to the audience about what's happening with the characters you've been watching. I suppose one could draw a parallel with song structure: The verses move the story forward, and the chorus tends to summarize the theme, to comment on the action. That sounds good. A chorus also is a mass of voices, as in a choir, which makes sense because the Greek chorus could sing or speak. And you're often expected to sing along with a song chorus, so it all ties together, right? That's my best guess, at any rate.

By the way, I'd never previously considered the Beatles' relationship to choruses. Some of their greatest songs have them, some not. "Let It Be": chorus. "Hey Jude": no chorus. "A Day in the Life" and "Yesterday": refrain, no chorus. "Strawberry Fields Forever" and "Penny Lane": chorus. "Revolution": chorus. "Norwegian Wood": no chorus. "Paperback Writer" appears to have a refrain *and* a chorus, the "paperback writer/paperback *writer!*" part at the end of each verse and then the multi-voiced "paperback writer" part that opens the song and repeats later.

As for the sound of a song, we definitely should explore this more later. But your comment about finding it difficult to enjoy a song if you don't like the voice made me think of the many singers to whom I had an initially negative reaction before eventually doing a 180. I bet I share this example with many: Elvis Costello. The first time I heard him, my reaction was *Wha'*? He was so adenoidal or nasal or whatever that strange quality to his voice was, with a pronounced vibrato and thick texture unlike anything else I'd heard. (If I'd been up on Graham Parker at the time, I might have been more acclimated.) I didn't like it. I made fun of it. Soon thereafter I loved it — because I loved his songs and what he was doing and thus him as an artist, and I also appreciated the power and expressiveness of his voice.

David Byrne is another one, or Andy Partridge from XTC, especially on the earlier albums when he had that hiccupping-walrus delivery. I suspect people have had similar reactions to Patti Smith and Chrissie Hynde. As you become more intimate with these singers' music, more connected to it, you come to think of them as your friends,

---

I'd never previously considered the Beatles' relationship to choruses. Some of their greatest songs have them, some not. "Let It Be": chorus. "Hey Jude": no chorus.

---

and you welcome hearing their voices almost apart from the aesthetic qualities. Partridge is never going to have the world's greatest voice, but it brings me far more pleasure than when I encounter, say, Rod Stewart, a more obviously gifted singer whose music, particularly post-early 1970s, rarely speaks to me.

We could wander down a long side path regarding whether singers tend to be the best interpreters of their own songs. We don't look to Cole Porter or George and Ira Gershwin or Rogers & Hammerstein for definitive performances of their classics; professional singers have taken ownership of them. The same goes for rock-era songwriters such as Leiber & Stoller or Bacharach & David or Goffin & King — except that Carole King eventually did lay claim to her own material. (Did you notice how I reflexively offered three examples in each case?) Rockers such as Buddy Holly, Carl Perkins and, as always, the Beatles — and soul singers such as James Brown, Smokey Robinson and Marvin Gaye (more 3's!) — really popularized the notion of the songwriter as singer, and the way popular-music culture has developed, we tend to forgive a lot of singer-songwriters' vocal quirks in the name of personal expression. As forcefully as Roger Daltrey delivers some of the Who's epic rockers, the songs sung by the thinner-voiced writer Pete Townshend may sound more "honest," no?

Do you think it's a requirement for songwriters to be able to perform their material ably?

As for repetition, when I was a kid and K.C. and the Sunshine Band's "That's the Way (I Like It)" would come on the radio, I used to try to count all of the "uh-huh"s. I recall the total was something like 94 — it was tough to get those last ones as the song faded out and the deejay started yapping. Now *that* was a lot of repetition. Should we stipulate that dance songs come with a different set of rules? If you told James Brown that he was allotted a mere three "Get up-a! (Get on up-a!)"s in "Get Up (I Feel Like Being a) Sex Machine," the song would be 11 seconds long. Musically as well as lyrically, funk is built around repetition, so let's set that aside.

I'm not the hugest Springsteen fan, but it never occurred to me to be bugged by all of those "down, down, down"s in "I'm Going Down." That's just the song, which certainly supports the notion that he's *really* going down. Seems akin to your not being bothered by the endless "small town" repetition in "Small Town." That's the song. So be it.

I remember going to a party many years ago, putting Elvis Costello's *This Year's Model* onto the turntable and trying to play "(I Don't Want To Go to) Chelsea," but I lowered the needle a bit early and landed on the previous track's coda, which goes like this: "Hand in hand! Hand in hand! Hand in hand! Hand in hand! Hand in hand! Hand in hand! Hand in hand! Hand in hand!" Someone there deadpanned, "Kind of repetitive, isn't it?" Well, now that you mention it...

Repetitions often come at the end of songs, particularly those that fade out, such as the Police's "Message in a Bottle": "Sending out an S.O.S. Sending out an S.O.S..." which my then-6-year-old consumer-minded daughter heard as "Spend it all, oh yes, oh yes..."

One of XTC's later songs, "Stupidly Happy," is basically a great lost Keith Richards riff beaten into the ground for more than four minutes. When I interviewed Andy Partridge some years back, he shared his disappointment that the song wasn't a worldwide smash; after all, he noted, "you're singing it before it's half over." My theory is that "Stupidly Happy" is a little *too* repetitive, especially given its length; the arrangement is constantly adding textures and intensity, but it still needs a break from that riff being drilled nonstop into your ear hole.

For Partridge this is an unusual problem because he's one of the most disciplined, structurally complex writers of catchy pop songs around. He almost always includes a bridge, even if it stretches the song beyond five minutes. Examples: "Senses Working Overtime" and "Towers of London," both great, both deserving of that elusive worldwide smashdom and both boasting killer bridges that lift the songs even higher. "Senses" also offers one of the all-time-fantastic sing-along choruses. My guess with "Stupidly Happy" is that his gut told him to keep it simple and just to build on that riff, not suspecting that the song might wind up spinning its wheels. Even the most riff-driven Rolling Stones songs, from "(I Can't Get No) Satisfaction" to "Start Me Up," have a lot of variation built in.

As a general rule I'd agree with you that it's probably better to repeat something too little than too much. If you want to hear that part you like one more time, *play the song again.* That's how it's supposed to work. This brings up a whole other topic: knowing when a song is done.

As far as I'm concerned, "Hey Jude" sustains its entire 7 minutes and 11 seconds, but plenty of other songs overstay their welcomes, the most egregious Beatles example perhaps being "It's All Too Much." I'd argue that R.E.M. lost its mojo not just when drummer-songwriter Bill Berry dropped out but also a bit previously, when the songs (and albums) began going on and on and on. Heck, I think even R.E.M.'s beloved "Man on the Moon" is one repeated bridge too long, but this trend really became pronounced on the bloated (if also at times inspired) *New Adventures in Hi-Fi* and continued in the post-Berry years until the final two comeback albums that, tellingly, featured leaner songs again.

So, Steve…

How do you know when a song has said all it needs to say and it's time to get out?

S   When is it time to call a song finished? Tough, very tough. Some songs feel like they are less finished than abandoned. I personally aim for an under-five-minute cap on my songs, with an average of about 3:30. I think going beyond five minutes is asking a lot from a listener unless there's something very cool going on. I personally do like the extended coda of "Hey Jude" because I dig the way Paul's voice breaks up and all the harmonics in his rasp, but I know quite a few people who despise that song. I also love the extended hypnotic drone of "Isn't It A Pity" with its echoes of "Hey Jude" and its meditation on man's inhumanity to man.

Dolly Varden tried something like that on *The Thrill of Gravity* with "The Old In and Out," a song about loss and disappointment. We recorded it all in one take. Mark Balletto's guitar playing was beautiful, and the band was really locked in. We intended to have it fade, but we all loved the development and ended up keeping it all. It clocks in at 6:38. Some people loved it; some hated it. That's probably the longest thing I've released, and it's barely even a song. The chorus is just "ahhh" and three simple verses. That felt right.

Oops: I just checked…. We had another song on that album called "The Wheels Have Left The Road" that is 8:43! Wow. That song is two verses, two choruses and a four-minute coda. People still request that song. Go figure.

I guess I'm seeing a pattern here I never recognized. There's a song on *The Panic Bell* called "Triumph Mine, Idaho" that is 6:59, and it is basically the same deal: The "song" part is 3:15, and the remaining nearly four minutes is an extended coda that builds and builds with a repeated couplet. If I were to play that song solo acoustic, or any of the three mentioned here, they'd be much shorter, and I would leave out much of the coda stuff because that's all about the band interacting. Band performance vs. song performance. So it's sort of a reaction to the song, in a way. As in: The song has been played; now let's sustain or heighten the mood as we interact for a few minutes. Maybe we're a jam band in hiding!

I tend to write two verses with a refrain or chorus and then ponder what to do next. Bridge? Third verse? I do love the challenge of writing a bridge, and it's where I can flex my harmony muscle skills a bit. A third verse can feel forced and redundant if there's no new idea or thought, and often this form…

Verse 1 + refrain

Verse 2 + refrain

Bridge

Repeat Verse 1 + refrain

...seems just fine. Either that or V1, Chorus, V2, Chorus, Bridge, repeat V1, Chorus.

I'm impressed by, and respect deeply Dylan's extended songs such as "Desolation Row" or "Tangled Up in Blue," but I couldn't do that, and I think nobody else really should either. It's all too much! I have a brand new song that has six very short little verses, but they are compound verses, meaning they're in pairs, so it's really three double verses and a chorus in between each pair. I really had to consider whether that was too much, but it feels right, and the whole thing clocks in around three minutes. I guess that, again, is the decision maker: How does it feel?

This is where having written, recorded and performed hundreds of songs over the past 30 years or so comes in handy. I have developed a sense of what works, what I like and what people will respond to. If I were mixing "The Old In and Out" today, would I fade it out before five minutes, or would I let it run its full length? I wonder.

I often tell songwriters in classes that they are the best singers of their songs. I've been hired by several people to sing their songs, which is nice, but I always tell them to give it a shot themselves. No one will sing your song quite the way you will. In pop and rock forms, having an idiosyncratic voice is actually a plus. As long as you can get close to being in tune, you're probably your best interpreter. There's been a bunch of albums of cover versions of Tom Waits songs, and I've found them all to be a bore. I'd much rather hear him sing 'em even though his voice is what it is. Same with Dylan, Neil Young, Patti Smith....

I've always dug Elvis Costello's voice so there was no getting used to that. I have a gut reaction against the singer from Death Cab For Cutie. I can't stand it. It gives me hives. I respect his writing, and they are a great band, but I can't listen to them. I don't know why; it's like an allergic reaction. Same with Eddie Vedder. Can't handle it, and I have to change the station. What's that about?

M   I can't help you with Eddie Vedder or Ben Gibbard (the Death Cab guy), though I don't share those allergies. Maybe Tom Waits could cover their songs? My musical Kryptonite used to be Geddy Lee or Bon Scott or, if I'm completely honest, Janis Joplin, but I've mellowed on all of them. I feel like I can get used to almost any voice, though when I don't like someone's songs, that poses a problem. I've had some difficulty with Caleb Followill and Kings of Leon for that reason, or maybe just because my sex *isn't* on fire.

As far as length goes, I revere the three-minute pop single, yet I also have a soft spot for some awfully long songs. Years ago I interviewed filmmaker Paul Thomas Anderson, and he was asserting that three-hour movies constitute their own genre, so something like *Boogie Nights* or *Magnolia* shouldn't be considered too long because, hey, they're in the three-hour-movie category. That may be circular reasoning, but you can make similar points with songs. "The Wheels Have Left the Road" fits in the category of **Song with Extended Coda**, which also would include "Hey Jude," "Isn't It a Pity," the original electric, non-sucky version of "Layla," "Free Bird" and lots of Richard Thompson songs ("If Love Whispers Your Name" being a relatively recent one). That's a valid category, so you can't knock it.

This is different from the **Jam Opus** category, which consists of less composed, more improvisatory songs by bands such as the Grateful Dead, Phish, the Allman Brothers, etc. This isn't really my thing, in part because I'm not a big fan of virtuosity for its own sake, but tight band interplay can be thrilling, even as it may be difficult to sit down and write out ahead of time. I'm more keen on the **Extended Funk Workout**, encompassing grooves built for the dance floor. Figure James Brown ("Sex Machine" et al) and Funkadelic on the early side, "Disco Inferno" somewhere in the middle and a whole industry of club remixes crowding today's output. You know what's a crazy-great Extended Funk Workout? "Halleluhwah" by the German "Krautrock" band Can. It's this tight bass-and-drums groove, with Japanese "singer" Damo Suzuki scatting nonsense on top, that sustains itself over a dizzying 18-and-a-half minutes. It gets my head bopping hard throughout — and it's from 1971 and has all of these mind-warping guitar effects and layered rhythms that presaged Talking Heads' ferociously groovy *Remain in Light* by nine years.

I'm not sure how useful that is in a songwriting discussion, but it's cool.

Let's move on to the **Prog Epic**, sometimes also known as the Big Wank (by me at least). Its heyday was the late '60s and early-mid '70s as bands devoted entire album sides to show-offy time signatures, hairpin turns, flamboyant musicianship, often-precious lyrics and an overarching pomposity. Is this fair? Do bands such as Yes, Genesis, King Crimson, Jethro Tull and Emerson, Lake & Palmer deserve such ridicule? Sometimes yes, sometimes no. (Re ELP: nodding head.) I enjoy some early Yes and Genesis songs — though they tend to be those rooted in pop values — and I don't think pretentiousness is automatically a bad thing. You want rock music to aspire to the artistic level of a symphony and poetry? Why not? Just be warned that when it doesn't work, it *really* doesn't work.

I guess **Dreamscapes** could be a category, though in general I don't consider ambient music to be songwriting per se. Pink Floyd incorporates Dreamscape elements, but I consider that band its own category as far as its long songs are concerned (and I'm talking primarily about their music, not lyrics). They have prominent guitar solos and can sound noodly at times, but Pink Floyd is no jam band; they're way too structured, controlled, intentional. They also ascended during the prog rock era and no doubt share fans with the artiest of those bands, yet they don't feel prog to me either, at least from *Meddle* onward. The music is too grounded, and it's never been about spotlighting chops aside from some David Gilmour guitar solos, and even those are more melodic and liquid-y than acrobatic. It's telling that one of the band's rare excursions into an off-kilter time signature, the 7/4 verses of "Money," came at the service of one of their catchiest, funkiest songs — and the shift to 4/4 kicks it into another gear.

I can't think of any other band that can pull off what Pink Floyd did, including Pink Floyd after Rogers Waters left and Waters himself. Maybe that's reason enough not to try to emulate them, as per your Dylan "Desolation Row"/"Tangled Up in Blue" edict. But I am fascinated by those Floydian Epics such as the side-long "Echoes" (dreamy Floyd, with dollops of "Across the Universe" thrown in), "Shine on You Crazy Diamond" (distinct, shimmering instrumental passages swelling to a lament about mind-fried band founder Syd Barrett) and perhaps my favorite, "Dogs." That one is 17 minutes long and covers almost the entire first side of *Animals*, yet is a carefully structured song with multiple sections as well as some droney stretches. It sustains a dark mood that balances beauty, ugliness and anger, and I find it captivating from start to finish.

The **Epic Ballad** category includes all of that long Dylan stuff plus countless folk songs ("Matty Groves," "The Wreck of the Edmund Fitzgerald"…). Another category might be called, simply, **Stretching Out**: songs set up as basic verse-chorus deals that just go on for quite a while, often thanks to extended instrumental interplay. Neil Young is an aficionado ("Down by the River," "Cortez the Killer," many more), and Television's tensely great "Marquee Moon" and some Wilco ("Misunderstood," "I Am Trying To Break Your Heard," "Spiders (Kidsmoke)") also would qualify.

And then we get to my favorite long-song genre: the **Pop Epic** — or, I suppose, Rock Epic, but I like the word "pop" in the gritty XTC "This is Pop" sense as opposed to the Katy Perry/Britney Spears disposable-plastic-dancey sense. These are lengthy because they have too many parts to squeeze into three minutes; their structure tends to be *this* and then *that* and then *this other thing* and then *that other thing* and so on. The Who's "A Quick One, While He's Away" may be the prototype, a 1966 exercise in scene shifting the goes from barbershop quintet to garage rock to soft-shoe shuffle to pre-punk sprint. It's not the most seamless piece of work, but it takes you on a fun ride. Green Day's rollicking "Jesus of Suburbia" wouldn't exist without it.

The Who continued in this vein with "Rael" (from *The Who Sell Out*) and chunks of *Tommy*. ("Won't Get Fooled Again" and "Who Are You," are more Stretching Out.) Paul McCartney is a Pop Epic master; "You Never Give Me Your Money" kind of set his template as it bounced from one idea to another, surging in energy and wrapping up in a mere four minutes, maybe too short to qualify for actual Pop Epic status. But almost all of side two of *Abbey Road* has a Pop Epic feel, and McCartney went on to craft such undeniable Pop Epics as the infectiously silly "Uncle Albert/Admiral Halsey," the understatedly sublime "Little Lamb Dragonfly," the exuberant "Band on the Run" and the arena-happy "Venus and Mars/Rock Show."

Queen's "Bohemian Rhapsody" is a career defining Pop Epic, and other notable ones include Radiohead's "Paranoid Android," Love's "You Set the Scene" (this one has made me weepy since I saw Arthur Lee perform it live with a full band and horn/string section), the Kinks' "Shangri-La" (a great lesser-known Ray Davies song) and Big Star's "O My Soul" (one of the most stripped-down, ramshackle Pop Epics around). Does Meat Loaf's "Paradise by the Dashboard Light" qualify? Um, yes. Is Styx's "Come Sail Away" a Pop Epic or a Prog Epic? Probably a Pop Epic, but I don't really care.

Anyway, this is a long way of saying that many great bands/artists have at least one epic in them, and epics often are viewed as bands' signature moments: Led Zeppelin's "Stairway to Heaven" or "Kashmir," the Who's "Won't Get Fooled Again," Dylan's "Like a Rolling Stone," the Beatles' "Hey Jude" or "A Day in the Life." So it's something to consider as a songwriter every once in a while. Could be a fun assignment, no? I personally would love to write the Next Great Pop Epic. We'll see.

OK, let's get back to a couple of concrete questions:

When do you know a song is done not in terms of length but in terms of making changes to it?

Are you editing and rewriting up to the moment you record? Are you still changing things as you perform it live? When, if ever, is the song set in stone?

Opening a different door…a lot of people co-write songs, but sometimes that means one person writes the lyrics and the other the music (Bernie Taupin and Elton John, Chris Difford and Glenn Tilbrook), and other times that means a variety of collaboration styles, either with a songwriting partner or an entire band.

What have been your best experiences in co-writing songs?

S   Some songs I'm still tinkering with as I'm tracking the final vocal. I'll try different words, play with the melody, or consider a chord change.

I attended a workshop with Darrell Scott, a great singer and songwriter (and guitarist) from Nashville, and he referred to his editing "tool box" for finishing songs. That box would be filled with everything he's learned as a musician and writer over the course of his life. I liked that, so I made a list of potential editing tools for my "Finish Your Damn Songs" class. Here's the list:

Lyrics Tools

Understanding of the English language

Ability to hear language as music, including syllable counting, stresses, rhyming and common vowel and consonant sounds

Vocabulary

Understanding of cultural references, clichés, colloquialisms, catch phrases and knowledge of existing song lyrics from all eras

Understanding of keys, what chords are in which keys and what their roles are

Understanding of major and minor tonalities and how to use them compositionally

How to get "out of the key" if desired

Knowledge of what notes are in which chords, what notes are consonant and what notes are dissonant and how to use that knowledge to make a stronger melody

Understanding song form and how to use it

Knowledge and competence with rhythm and how to find the right feel, tempo and spaciousness for your song

Competence on the instrument of your choice

Once a song is recorded and released, I consider it finished — most of the time. On rare occasions I'll come up with a new idea for a song that I think would make it better after it's been recorded and released and want to adjust it for playing live. The band is never happy about that.

I'm realizing more and more the benefit of firm deadlines and their ability to help with the creative process. Without a deadline we'd always be "in process," which would be fun, but there would be no output. I *love* recording. I love trying new sounds, instruments, moving parts around, etc. It's sometimes really sad to make a final mix and to call a song "finished." I hear people say in class all the time that without the writing assignment deadlines, they wouldn't write a single song. I suppose I'm always looking to the next project — a new album or "big" concert — with an eye on the new material I'll be presenting. Then I'll make a schedule backwards based on how many songs I might need and figure in time to write and record them. By doing that I make my own self-imposed deadlines to keep myself productive.

I wonder if suddenly someone told me I could never perform or record new songs again whether I would continue to write. Part of me thinks I would because I enjoy it, and songs tend to appear whether I want them to or not, but I don't know whether I'd bother to write them down and put them into a "fixed" state. A big part of writing songs, I believe, is a desire to communicate with others. Music is very deeply embedded in our primitive consciousness. It speaks to us on a level beyond language and explanation. From my earliest memories I was obsessed with music and wanted to get inside it and feel some sense of how in the world it worked. In a big way I still feel that. The other part, though, is I wanted to

— and continue to want to — make other people feel the way I felt when I listened to music as a kid and teenager. It made the world make a bit more sense and gave me context and an outlet for emotions and just made me happy. So that's the sharing aspect.

I'm sure there's a pretty big narcissistic element in there too: Listen to *me*! I remember a very good musician friend talking about his thoughts on why we all want to make records. He said we all want a bit of immortality. I think that's true. We all want to feel that we matter and that we'll be remembered for something good, maybe even something great. There's a interview with Randy Newman in *Songwriters on Songwriting* where he talks about aiming to write the best song that's ever been written each time he writes. Even if it's for a fleeting moment, he says he thinks it's important for songwriters to aim for the ultimate brass ring and to have the courage and ego to think they can do it. I have felt that way from time to time. The feeling goes away very quickly, of course, but it can drive the process.

So, for me, all those things combine and make me want to continue creating songs and recordings, and that means I have to finish the songs. Some songs are obviously finished, and some have to be worked and worked on. At some point, though, if I've created a firm deadline, I have to make a decision either to call it finished or to abandon it. That's the magic of the deadline. I'm very much in the "keep or abandon" stage

The goal is to be as open and honest with the other person as you would be with yourself.

right now as we're in the final stage of making a new record with Dolly Varden. I have 14 songs that will probably be whittled down to 12. One of them I had already abandoned until one of the band members brought it up and made me give it another chance. Now I like it again. When you get so close to a project, it's very difficult to know anything with absolute certainty. I'm trying to learn to trust my gut instincts rather than to get caught up in what others say or what my own insecurities might tell me.

On another topic you raised, I never listened to "prog" rock at all growing up. I only had my dad's records and a country radio station in Idaho, and both of those were prog-free zones. My dad and stepmom

had classic rock (Beatles, Stones), singer-songwriters (Neil Young, Dylan,
James Taylor), some decent soul and R&B (Marvin Gaye, Stevie Wonder) and jazz. The radio station was Kenny Rogers and Juice Newton, more or less. Late at night sometimes I could get a "modern" rock station from Salt Lake City that broadcast the hits of the early '80s. Anyway, I never really heard prog until college, probably, and I never "got" Yes. Too complicated! I've tried more recently, and I sure appreciate the musicianship, but it does absolutely nothing for me.

I can't stand Pink Floyd. I like the Syd Barrett stuff 'cause it's weird and creative, but the post-Barrett stuff, to me, is bloated, pompous and boring. Sorry about that! I've tried so hard to like them! I honestly could care less about fancy blues/rock guitar playing, so whoever the guitarist is in P. Floyd makes no impression on me. He's good, yep, but I don't care. I'd much rather listen to Freddy King or Link Wray or Keith Richards or Chuck Berry. But they have millions and millions of hard-core fans, so obviously I'm in the wrong...

Co-writing is really, really, really hard. I've had very limited success with it, and I still feel like I don't completely understand it. My best success has been with a singer/songwriter from Baltimore named Ellen Cherry. We've written a few very nice songs together from scratch face-to-face. The goal is to be as open and honest with the other person as you would be with yourself. As with any relationship, that is very difficult. You have to want to share your best ideas and be open to having them questioned and/or rejected. That goes for both people.

I think with most of the great rock writing duos — Mick and Keith, John and Paul — they were rarely starting the songs face-to-face. One person would come in with a solid idea or even a nearly completed song, and the other person would flesh it out or add something. In the case of Keith Richards, I think he mostly came up with the guitar parts and maybe a hook line of lyrics, and Mick finished the lyrics and shaped the song. John and Paul wrote songs from scratch together very early on, but by *A Hard Day's Night* they were writing separately and getting together to shape them and finish them. Elton and Bernie had a fascinating writing relationship where they were never face-to-face while writing. Bernie left the lyric sheets on Elton's piano, and Elton would work through them on his own.

Diane and I wrote one song completely together in Stump The Host, "Vacation In Des Moines," about visiting her parents in Iowa. It was fun and silly and required no "deep" thoughts. For her songs she'll usually write the melody and words, and I'll help her with the chords since she has a limited knowledge of guitar and theory. I can add underpinnings to her beautiful melodies that she might not come up with. That's much more craft-based than inspiration-based. She will occasionally suggest a lyric change to one of my songs that makes it better, and in those cases I give her a writing credit.

In Nashville co-writing is the rule, and it seems to me its closest comparison would be the creative process used by advertising agencies: a group of people gathered with the goal of selling an idea, through song, to a targeted demographic. There's a fixed set of limitations, a group of creative people who have the tools and knowledge needed and a goal of making a sellable product. That's fine, I suppose. Just listen to country radio, and you'll hear what the result of that is. For me, it's not a process I can embrace.

M   For the record you're not wrong about Pink Floyd because they have millions and millions of hard-core fans. So does Nickelback. So does Britney Spears. So does *Two and a Half Men*. Taste isn't up for a majority vote; we're allowed to like what we like and dislike what we dislike.

No, you're wrong about Pink Floyd because they actually have some very cool post-Barrett songs despite others that fit your "bloated, pompous" description. So there.

I agree with you about deadlines. As a daily newspaper journalist, I'm already inclined to work under time pressure, and songwriting-wise I never was as productive as I was when taking your classes. I have many songs that have remained unfinished for years, but with the expectation of presenting a newly completed work to fellow songwriters each week, I was knocking them out and liking them as much as anything else I'd written, even as I occasionally was able to repurpose some song parts I had lying around. And it's not like I put so much more effort into the ones that take longer; it's more like I've procrastinated in applying the same intense focus to those songs as I did to the class ones. Intense focus — that's the key.

Deadlines actually played a key role in one of my few song-writing collaborations. Many years ago my friend Ted and I retreated to a vacation-home basement with his four-track cassette recorder, guitars, a microphone and a keyboard into which you could insert discs to program different sounds. We'd first insert the disc that turned the keys into different percussion sounds, and then we'd pound out some sort of rhythm, each of us on a different part of the keyboard. We might add another percussion track or two, then mix them all down. After that we'd add a bass line (on the keyboard again) and a guitar track, so now the thing would have chords. We might add other sounds after that — electric piano, harpsichord, faux strings, monk-like choir — and then I'd come up with the melody and words.

The first song was a simple sub-Stonesy groove with lyrics that didn't go much beyond, "Got to get away now/'Cause I got to got to get away…" The second one, "Disc Error," was inspired by a hitch in the keyboard's percussion disc that created a weird click-and-woo effect that gave the song some fun syncopation. I wrote pun-filled lyrics about a guy who can't connect, and Ted sang them with impressive passion. ("I want to interface/But I've got a disc error/My drive is not in place/I've got a disc error.") For the third one, I took a title that I'd stowed in my mental hip pocket, "When I Look Into Your Eyes (I See Your Eyes)," and wrote a set of lyrics that I thought actually stood up in a real song-song sort of way. But the key was that while I was upstairs writing the words, Ted was waiting in the basement, so I had to get them done pronto. Deadline.

I was reading Paul Myers' book about Todd Rundgren, *A Wizard a True Star*, and it describes how Rundgren, working solo or with his band Utopia, would lay down all of the instrumental tracks before writing the lyrics or even concocting the vocal melody — so I guess Ted and I were working in the Rundgren method. Rundgren said he took this approach on every album starting with *Something/Anything*, saying he'd have "only a vague idea what (the song) would be about and possibly no lyrics at all until it would be time to sing it. Then I'd start singing along with the track, trying to find melodies to go along with it, and eventually words would start coming." Such a strategy must lend some urgency to the process while forcing you to finish the song, at least if you want to be able to move on to the next one.

Ted and I made up just five songs together, and the last one was the trickiest. We had a kind of the Coasters-go-tropical vibe going, and when we were done with the instrumental bed, we each had a different idea of what should go on top. Ted wanted it to be a sort of drony chant that accentuated the rhythm. I came up with a melody that was really tuneful and covered a lot of ground, and in my stubborn songwriter way I *knew* it was the right thing for this song. I proposed that we use his part as the backdrop to my part, and I headed upstairs to bang out the lyrics. This one became "Mrs. Gorilla," as inspired by a big stuffed animal in the room, though the lyrics were more about a fellow confused by love. We wound up agreeing that "Mrs. Gorilla" was our best song of the bunch — despite the fact that it was a song called "Mrs. Gorilla" — and we never wrote another one together.

Why didn't this collaboration last? Because, I think, at the beginning we had no idea what our roles were, and we were both excited to add what we could add, and it felt even. But as we continued, we had more definite, divergent opinions about where the songs should go, and for two musical Alpha Males, this dynamic was not sustainable. It was too bad, though — I like those songs.

I have so many unfinished songs that you'd think I would seek out a collaborator, but as a word guy in the professional part of my life, I can't abide letting someone else handle the lyrics. I've had a friend or two suggest I finish incomplete songs of theirs as well, but I've never been able to get into the right mindset. Maybe I haven't tried hard enough.

That said, I do enjoy the recording process and hearing how other musicians flesh out what I've written. You're experienced in this area:

How does a band dynamic affect songwriting?

Do you tell the bassist what to play, or does Mike come up with his own parts? What about the drummer (Matt) or lead guitarist (Mark) — do you suggest their contributions or let the arrangements grow organically? And is there a requirement that all Dolly Varden members who aren't you or Diane have an M name? Should I join?

Finally, if a band member comes up with a great little riff or countermelody, does he get a songwriting credit, or is that part of his job of being in a band? How do you balance songwriting and collaboration, and at what point do you say, "No, I'm the songwriter, and the song must go like *this*?"

S   Interesting. I'm amazed that those Todd Rundgren songs were tracked as music first. I just don't see how that's possible. Paul Simon's *Graceland* and the one after it (*The Rhythm of the Saints*) were done that way, too — whole tracks finished before he began adding words and melody. That's an amazing amount of confidence in the form. My friend Jason Narducy (Verbow) writes this way mostly. He and I kicked some songs ideas around recently for a new album he's working on for a new band called Split Single. He does have melodies from the beginning, though: chords, a groove and a melody. Words come last. I always have to have words pretty early in the process, or I don't feel like continuing to work on the song.

Yes, being in a band is certainly a form of collaboration. I've always tried to work with musicians with whom I get along musically. I'd say most of the time the process works this way: I come in with a new song that has chords, words and melody, and I play it on acoustic guitar for the band. I tell them the chords, and we start to run through it trying out different drum patterns, dynamics, places for Diane to sing, places for Mark to play guitar lines. Sometimes that process works immediately, and sometimes we flail around for weeks or months trying to find the right setting. If it's a difficult one to work out with the band, then we'll all make suggestions — sometimes benign, sometimes heated.

That stuff, though, I would call "arranging," not songwriting. The song is finished before I play it for the band for the first time. Maybe I haven't completed all the words, or a chord might change, but for the most part the songwriting is complete. Occasionally someone will make a suggestion that changes the structure of the song itself, or Mark will add a riff that becomes a signature part of the song, or Diane will suggest some lyric changes. In those cases they get a songwriting credit. Otherwise it's arranging. That's how I see it at least.

On very rare occasions I've written a song while the band was just improvising a groove. Then it's a bit of a grey area. When we worked with producer Brad Jones in Nashville (*The Dumbest Magnets* and *Forgiven Now*), he made significant changes to some of the songs. He deleted verses, added instrumental bridges, changed chords and more. I felt that he should get songwriting credit in those cases, but he declined, saying that to him that all fell under the "producer" job description.

I have one recollection from recording *Magnets* that's worth sharing. I had made a demo of the song "I Come To You" that was a big mess. I was uncomfortable with the song because it seemed so simple. I was unsure if it was even worth recording. Brad said, "I love that song, and if I heard someone singing it on just acoustic guitar at an open-mic night, it would still be great." That was what I needed to convince me to record it, and now it's one of the very most popular and enduring Dolly Varden songs. Songwriters aren't always the best judges of their own work and need that outside perspective, which is what a good producer can provide.

M   Would that "arranging, not songwriting" dynamic apply your work with your more jazz-oriented band, Funeral Bonsai Wedding, as well. Your songs no doubt are "written," but that group's self-titled album and live performances have more of a loose, improvised feel than the music you've made with Dolly Varden or solo.

When a song's blueprint becomes the basis for jamming or improvising, where do you draw the line between songwriting and arranging?

S   Well, gosh, that's a good question. I've always been in bands that basically play fleshed out versions of the song as written on acoustic guitar. In a way, Funeral Bonsai Wedding is no different; it's just that all three of those musicians (Jason Adasiewicz on vibraphone, Frank Rosaly on drums and Jason Roebke on upright bass) have such distinct, unique musical personalities that the music sounds unlike anything else. I consciously wrote those songs with fewer chord changes and more open spaces than usual to give them chances to stretch out a bit. So I guess that's songwriting with arranging in mind.

In most cases the open spaces are breaks between verses where the tonic is held as a drone of sorts, allowing for any color to be added for a semi-determined amount of time until the next verse begins. In live performance we've been experimenting with improvised transitions between the songs themselves, and that has been really fun and exciting. The thing that is different in Funeral Bonsai Wedding's case is that they aren't "parts" per se. So that's neither songwriting nor arranging, I guess. The "arrangement" is the agreement that at certain specific points in the song, the band will stretch out. There is a basic blueprint, but what they play on a particular song is always a little bit different.

So the versions on the album are just one version of the song, not *the* version of the song. I consciously try to not sing them the same way each time, too. The lyrics are pretty set, but the phrasing differs from performance to performance. These songs are challenging to listen to, I think. Some people have really been moved by the album, but the response seems to be less positive overall than the last Dolly Varden album, *For A While*.

I read again and again that writers are surprised by which of their songs become popular. I know in my case that the ones people respond to aren't always the ones I think are my best work. I also think that people don't actually become better songwriters the longer they do it. Look at Springsteen, McCartney, Dylan, Stevie Wonder, geez, almost everyone. The work they did in their 20s and 30s was their best. There could be a lot of reasons for that. It's a scary premise, though, as I'm well past those years too.

I like to think I'm getting better at this — better at letting ideas flow and finding interesting music settings. I'm certainly a better musician now than I was 10 years ago. You absolutely can become a better musician through the miracle of practice! I do think that with songwriting the longer you work at it, the more you become comfortable with the process. I know what it feels like when a good song is arriving, and I know to stick with it. I have a bigger bag of crafting tools than I had 10 or 15 years ago, and I'm open to trying new things.

Can you think of many songwriters who have gotten better and better well into their careers?

M   Ah, the dreaded age question. Beethoven was 53 and almost completely deaf when he completed his Ninth Symphony, Giuseppe Verdi was 60 when he debuted his *Requiem* and 73 when his opera *Otello* premiered. But they weren't rockers.

Orson Welles may be the poster child for filmmakers who peaked early, and Francis Ford Coppola never approached his incredible 1970s run of films (*The Godfather*, *The Conversation*, *The Godfather Part II* and *Apocalypse Now*, made when he was in his 30s). But Alfred Hitchcock's most celebrated stretch came when he was in his 50s (in the 1950s), and Clint Eastwood directed best picture winners *Unforgiven* and *Million Dollar Baby* when he was 62 and 74, respectively. Fyodor Dostoyevsky's greatest work was his last, *The Brothers Karamazov*, completed when he was 59 — and back then 59 was *old*. (It certainly was to him; he died four months later.)

So what's the deal with rock music? Why do rock songwriters generally do better work when they're still learning their craft than after they've accumulated more skill and life experience?

Does inspiration have a shelf life?

Although McCartney kept making pretty strong albums into his early 70s, none of those later songs are indelible in the way that his earlier, more celebrated work was. Elvis Costello remains a master craftsman, but are his newer songs vital and *necessary* the way his older ones were? And is this solely a function of the music or also related to a fan base that (a) has aged along with him and may value music in a less passionate way than it did when *Imperial Bedroom* came out, and (b) has been inundated with so much Costello music over the years that almost nothing he does can feel completely new anymore, even if it's actually just as strong? If *Momofuku* had come out right after *Blood and Chocolate*, would it have felt more essential?

And how much of this is a matter of age versus productivity? McCartney, Costello, Prince, etc., wrote so many songs over the years that at some point you wonder how many melodies or ideas they could have left. Can we really expect lightning to keep striking McCartney? Hasn't it struck enough?

Yet there are some counterexamples. I wrote a *Chicago Tribune* story about the power-pop band Shoes releasing its first new album in 18 years, and the shocking part for me was that *Ignition* sounds stronger and fresher than what they were doing before their hiatus. The three almost-60-year-old singer-songwriters, Gary Klebe and Jeff and John Murphy, told me they hadn't been writing songs over all of those years; they got down to the composing and arranging only after they decided to make a new album a couple of years earlier. Would I have been able to tell the difference between songs that had been kicking around for a dozen years versus newly written ones? Who knows?

But it's not like their material reflects even semi-current musical trends like hip hop or EDM. This is classically structured, Beatles-influenced, guitar-led, harmonies-infused melodic rock, intended to be timeless if never groundbreaking. And with the band on just its eighth studio album since 1976, and with the three key members sharing the writing equally, none of them has composed all that many songs. Maybe, age aside, their creative wells simply have yet to be drained.

Then again, the norm is for groups, prolific or not, to lose their steam after many years and/or long layoffs. Some of that may be age related, though stage of life may be just as large a factor. Younger people tend to be more driven and passionate than older folks; is that because they physically have more energy or because they haven't started families or otherwise rearranged their priorities? Here's another thought: Younger people tend to be more confused and troubled, a combination that may make for better songs than having figured more things out and finding some semblance of contentment. Also, twentysomething angst may be more widely relatable than fortysomething or fiftysomething angst, at least in rock, with its emphasis on love songs and youthful rebellion. At the same time, though, there's something to be said for the wisdom of accumulated years, no?

What I too often find lacking in older musicians is urgency; few things are more depressing than seeing a veteran band or artist straining to recapture the energy and sound of earlier work. Then again,

McCartney was 57 upon the 1999 release of *Run Devil Run*, his first album after his wife Linda died, and it rocked as passionately as any of his solo work, and his cover of Dickie Bishop and the Sidekicks' "No Other Baby" is one of his great performances/interpretations. (He sounded even more wild and unhinged on his 2008 Fireman album, *Electric Arguments*.) Dylan had accumulated 56 years and an awful lot of songs by the time he released *Time Out of Mind* (1997), and I love that album; it's music he couldn't have recorded in his 20s. What may be Richard Thompson's most beloved song, "1952 Vincent Black Lightning," came out when he was 42, and he has written many indelible songs since. Neil Young keeps throwing cranky curve balls into his 70s. So there's hope.

I like the Shoes example because here I am, a middle-aged dude, continuing to work on songs even though I've never done anything concrete with any of them. Do I think my newer songs are weaker than those I wrote in my 20s? Probably not, because I have taken my sweet time (to say the least) to develop my craft, thus allowing myself much room to grow. I also have songs that I started in my 20s that I'm just getting around to finishing now, so what's their age stamp? Does it matter?

Maybe or maybe not. It's not like there's much precedent for someone at my relatively advanced age to launch a successful music career, anyway. Then again, to excel in music, you've got to be exceptional somehow, so why not be exceptional in an age-defying way? A guy can dream…

As for you, you strike me as someone who's in that Richard Thompson camp; your work is consistently strong and steady, and you have yet to release an album with material that doesn't stand proudly among its predecessors. The newest Dolly Varden album contains a few of your very best songs (everyone reading this should listen to "Mayfly" right now), so you're not washed up yet.

I bet it helps that you're constantly engaged in the world and your craft; you perform all the time with different musicians, you teach lessons and classes, and you're out living an active life. I get the feeling that a lot of writers — famous ones, at least — dry up because they're not doing that much anymore; massive success buys some folks too much down time. This would be an interesting study: Do musicians who work steadily without hitting the so-called big time have more consistent long-term careers, at least in terms of inspiration, than those who become rich and famous out of the box?

We also haven't talked about the influence of drugs and alcohol, which I'd guess has been a factor in the lives of many of the songwriters we've discussed here. I've often wondered whether the fact that so many rock musicians have gone through druggy/drinking periods has had an effect on their longevity as creative artists, just as William Faulkner's alcoholism is often cited in relation to the drop-off in quality of his later work. Obviously there are plenty of examples of musicians who flamed out early while under the influence (Syd Barrett, Brian Wilson…though Wilson continued making music).

At the same time, some musicians credit drugs and alcohol with spurring their creativity; this argument may have been most prominent when the Beatles were admitting to dropping acid around the time of their psychedelic landmark *Sgt. Pepper's Lonely Hearts Club Band*. In the Todd Rundgren book I mentioned earlier, he discusses how he never did drugs up till his album *A Wizard, a True Star*, which he wrote and recorded while experimenting with psychedelics. Some of that album is brilliant; other parts are juvenile and borderline unlistenable. He also discusses smoking pot to loosen him up artistically.

Being under the impression that you've never wrestled with a substance abuse habit, I'd say the prognosis is good for you to continue to be creative as you become an even older fart than you already are. But what are your thoughts about giving your creativity a little boost through artificial means?

Do you ever have a drink or do anything else to help get the juices flowing?

You've been around plenty of musicians over the years; do you think this sort of thing helps in the short or long term?

S   Hoo, boy, that's a tough topic. Famous drug-abusing songwriters like James Taylor and David Crosby say they *might* have written the same songs had they not been high, but they can't say for sure. George Harrison was pretty certain that he wouldn't have come up with many of his late '60s songs without the influence and mind expansion of LSD. It is very hard to imagine John Lennon writing "Tomorrow Never Knows" without acid.

Here's what I think: Creativity comes from the place in our brains where dreams originate. That is a very open, uninhibited and non-logical place. Artists *can* get to that "zone" naturally, and that's what I've been talking about during this conversation, and that's what I teach in my classes. Some artists find a controlled substance can help get them to that dreaming/waking state. The natural method is frustrating, and often nothing comes of it. Patience is very much required. Drugs can get you there, or they can make you *think* you've gotten there.

The danger, of course, is addiction. James Taylor has said he would trade all the songs he wrote while high to never have been addicted to heroin. Some artists die of alcohol poisoning, too. Let's not leave drinking out! I love to get drunk and sing. I can't say I've ever written anything good while under the influence of drugs or alcohol, though it's not something I've made a habit of. I don't know whether musicians are particularly susceptible to addiction, but there certainly have been a lot of drug- and alcohol-related deaths in the world of music. Then again, there are famous pot smokers like Louis Armstrong (who is reported to have been high every day of his adult life) and Willie Nelson; both had or have thriving careers into their old age, and Art Blakey was a heroin addict his entire professional life, and he lived to be 71. But there are many more sad stories of people dying from drug-related causes well before their time: Jimi Hendrix, Janis Joplin, Brian Jones, Charlie Parker, Gram Parsons and so many more.

I think that artists in general are an insecure bunch and that getting high can be a tonic. It can also very quickly become a crutch. That's my personal experience with musicians who've had issues with drugs and alcohol. It becomes sad and unworkable pretty fast. The addiction overtakes the artistry, and then you're just dealing with someone who needs help. The image of the rock musician getting high and making an incredible record is cool, but the reality of that same person becoming a pathetic drug addict is something to consider. Would Hendrix say it was worth it? I don't know. Keith Richards made no apologies in his book for his years of drug taking. He is a rare one. For a young teenager who wanted to be a rock 'n' roll singer, the photo in *Exile on Main Street* where Keith and Mick are singing together both holding bottles of booze was pretty potent.

Neil Young, in addition to continuing to create new stuff into his '70s, seemed to have worked under the influence of pot and alcohol off and on over his career. For him it worked as one way of creating, at least until he finally stopped. I guess George Harrison would say the same thing: It worked at the time for what he was doing, but he found he had to move away from it to have a fuller life.

One thing I've always disliked, though, is the knee jerk reaction of people who say, "He must have been on drugs to come up with that!" I think it's a pop-culture romantic notion to think that you have to be high to come up with really imaginative work. Some very original and mind-expanding work has come from people who are absolutely drug free. It's a sign of our collective distrust of creativity and the creative process that so many people suppose that you have to be wasted to come up with original work. It's a romantic notion that is reinforced by the music industry, too, and that is sad.

One last thing about aging and creativity... I mentioned that I'm well into my 40s in songwriting class recently. I guess I am fortunate that I look younger that I am, so I often surprise people when I tell them my age. This particular class was mostly dudes in their 40s, and we got into a discussion about how we all wish we'd had our 40-year-old brains when we were in our 20s. There is a beautiful freedom that occurs sometime after 40 where you slowly stop caring about the little bullshit things that used to make you miserable. The ability to not give a shit is a beautiful, freeing thing. That's not to say I care less about my writing or singing. I find that I just don't let the day-to-day bothersome stuff drag me down as much as I used to. That stuff is such a huge waste of emotional time. For me, I think, it has made me a better writer because I can really write for myself and feel confident that I'm doing what I should be doing rather than worrying about what someone might think.

I saw Stephen King on a talk show, and he admitted that he no longer cares if anyone likes his books or if they even bother to read them. I think that's the same thing we were talking about in class. It's not that he doesn't put all his best effort into writing the books; it's just that when the writing and editing are finished, he's done with them and on to the next thing. You may or may not care for his writing, but that's not the point. The point is that artists who've grown into their work as they've aged begin to have that sense of purpose and freedom without needing approval.

That's sort of where I'm finding myself lately, and it feels really good. I think young people need a lot of approval, whether they say so or not, and that desperation can be attractive in some cases and repulsive in others. Or maybe even a little of both at the same time! Rock and roll thrives on that youthful passion and desperation, and it is an incredible rush. I think that's why the crop of aging classic rockers leaves us wanting. It's just weird to see old folks trying to recreate their youthful passion and desperation. Elvis Costello is a perfect example for me. It's weird to see him sing those old songs — even though he sounds great and always has a great band. Am I an ageist?

No, you're not an ageist. I think the litmus test regarding such questions is believability, otherwise known as the "Should the Who keep playing 'My Generation'?" conundrum. Did you know that when Roger Daltrey sang *Quadrophenia* on the Who's fall 2012 tour, he was the same age that Jack Lemmon was when *Grumpy Old Men* came out? Sure, he could still stutter, "I hope I d-d-die before I get old," but at this point the song plays as ironic commentary, especially given that the band's rhythm section did exactly that. When I saw the Beach Boys in 1992, 51-year-old Mike Love sang "Be True to Your School" amid nubile cheerleaders waving their pom-poms; the whole effect was *ecchh*. More than two decades later, he was still singing it. Yet there's something poignant about 70something Brian Wilson singing "God Only Knows" in the 2010s, and when he plays "Till I Die," it's devastating. So, yeah, although their surfin'/hot-roddin' songs now feel like little more than nostalgia, the more deeply felt ones hold up fine.

Likewise, McCartney may no longer be credible singing, "Well, she was just 17/You know what I mean" (though "I Saw Her Standing There" is such a sturdy rocker, he can be forgiven even for that), but you can't imagine him *not* singing "Let It Be" or "Hey Jude," and those later Beatles songs are almost a half century old. When I saw Arthur Lee and Love perform the wonderful acoustic-orchestral 1967 album *Forever Changes* in its entirety in 2003, I was knocked out by the finale, "You Set the Scene," as Lee — then in his late 50s, recently out of prison on a gun charge and a bit nuts — delivered his twentysomething musings on mortality: "This is the only thing that I am sure of/And that's all that lives is gonna die/And there'll always be some people here to wonder why…" The words had come to mean something different given all that he'd been through, and they struck me differently too as I was much older than I was when I'd discovered the album in college. Lee died three years later of leukemia, lending the song even more potency.

I suspect your problem with Costello on those earlier songs is that he's affecting a persona you no longer buy as credible. He's not the angry young man of *This Year's Model* anymore, so when he starts spewing the bile, it can feel like an act. Then again, he'd moved beyond that defiant stance by album No. 4 (*Get Happy!!*), so for the most part I'm fine with him mixing the old and the new; the craftsmanship holds up. It just so happens that his impassioned cover of Nick Lowe's "(What's So Funny 'Bout) Peace, Love and Understanding" now resonates more than his caustic "Radio Radio." This is another reason Dylan's approach makes sense: If song interpretations are ever-evolving, then you never sound like an old man imitating a young man.

Your point about the freedom of not giving a shit is a great one and in many ways should trump those concerns about age. When I was writing a local music column way back when, the up-and-coming rockers invariably would tell me their goals were to get signed by a major label and to play for a lot of people — that is, to become rich and famous. Those are relatable goals, but often you could hear how those values were shaping the music, as the musicians smoothed out their idiosyncrasies and jettisoned much of what might have made them unique. Those compromises rarely paid off. The artists who succeeded tended to be the ones who stubbornly followed their own muses. So, yeah, better to get those concerns, calculations and self-consciousness off the table. When you're not counting on becoming a rock star or even making a living through songs — because, really, how many people can do that anymore? — you're liberated to create the music *you* most want to hear.

As for the drug discussion, I remember my college girlfriend once saying to me: "You have the druggiest musical taste of any non-druggy person I know." I've always enjoyed psychedelia, particularly the intersection of trippy and poppy (Pink Floyd's *The Piper at the Gates of Dawn*, "Strawberry Fields Forever"/"A Day in the Life"/"I Am the Walrus," "Eight Miles High" and any number of songs that employed

It does seem like people who don't fry their minds enjoy more creative longevity.

phase shifts and sitars) as opposed to drawn-out jams (i.e. I was never a Dead fan). This stuff just works for me musically — I love the anything-goes approach to sounds and arrangements within the strictures of melodic songwriting — and one shouldn't have to be in an altered state to compose in this genre or to appreciate it. If you must be stoned to enjoy a certain piece of music, to me that's a sign it may not be so good.

And, yes, I'm glad Lennon had whatever experiences he had to inspire "Tomorrow Never Knows" and the great psychedelic songs to follow, but I also wonder about the strong material he might have written had he not gotten into hard drugs and eventually become hooked on heroin, albeit apparently briefly. Think about how creative and dominant he was up through *Rubber Soul* — or even on The White Album, with most of his material composed while he was relatively clean in India — and then look at the *Let It Be* sessions when he was strung out, struggled to come up with much usable material and, if you believe reported accounts, left McCartney and his bandmates to do much of the arranging. Would McCartney have towered over the late Beatles had Lennon's head been in the game as much? Even in his solo career, Lennon never pushed boundaries like he did before he dove deeply into drugs (and apparently drank an awful lot). I have no idea whether these two points actually are related — his resistance to rock stardom also may have been a factor, he'd lost some powerful collaborators, and he'd already innovated an awful lot — but it does seem like people who don't fry their minds enjoy more creative longevity. Then again, your example of Neil Young is a good counterpoint; he wrote in his 2012 memoir, *Waging Heavy Peace*, that he was stoned when he made every album before that year's rejuvenating excursions with Crazy Horse.

I do understand the desire to free one's mind from its usual rigidity. Sometimes when I'm writing lyrics, I feel like I'm working on a math problem as I look for the perfect rhyme and try to make the meter work. We talked about this earlier, the way that songwriting can feel like an intellectual exercise rather than an intuitive creative endeavor. Yet one of the things that I think blocks up a lot of people is the fear of clichés. Most songs are about love, yet at some point love feels like a cliché. And then there's the word "love" and how if you end a line on it, you start thinking about "stars above" and "thinking of" and "like a glove." Chord changes and melodies also can be cliché minefields; you go to the IV or V chord or come up with three notes that sound familiar together, and your brain starts rebelling: "No, no, no!" A friend who's an accomplished guitarist and bassist told me recently he gave up songwriting because he felt like everything he wrote was a cliché.

You stressed earlier that people should not shun basic chord changes, but:

What's your feeling about clichés in general? Avoid them? Go with them?

Use them in the first draft and try to substitute something better later?

S

I've had a complete change of mind about clichés in songs. When I started teaching songwriting, I went with the standard creative writing dictum of: Avoid clichés at all costs. Then I read an *A.V. Club* interview with Stephin Merritt of the Magnetic Fields in which he said that not only does he not have any clichés he tries to avoid, but when he spots one, he goes for it. He called clichés "the most useful thing in songwriting...the tool on which you build the rest of the song" — although rhyming "dance" with "romance" might be pushing it even for him.

As I thought about this, I realized that the entire history of great songwriting is based on using clichés, colloquialisms, figures of speech, etc, as *the* thing to build a song around. I mentioned earlier Keith Richards' appreciation of a good phrase. Then you consider: "Under My Thumb," "Heart of Stone," "Let's Spend the Night Together," "You Can't Always Get What You Want," "It's Only Rock 'n' Roll," "Wild horses couldn't drag me away." Then you think back to Tin Pan Alley and, wow, it's cliché-o-rama. Look at the Irving Berlin catalog ("Better Luck Next Time," "I'm Putting All My Eggs in One Basket," "There's No Business Like Show Business," for starters) or Ira Gershwin ("Let's Kiss and Make Up," "My One and Only," "The Man That Got Away"...). It's either common clichéd phrases or quippy wordplay based on a common saying. I noticed that there's an Ira Gershwin song called "Isn't It A Pity?" So that one worked twice!

Song titles, by the way, are not copyright protected. Classic country songs are filled with clichés, especially when you can take a well-known phrase and flip it on its head or make it have a double meaning. Songs of Harlan Howard include "Above and Beyond The Call (of Love)" and "Pick Me Up (on Your Way Back Down)."

One that I used is "It's Not What You Think" (from my solo album *I Will Miss the Trumpets and the Drums*). I think I wrote that after I read the Merritt interview. I tried to keep the phrase ambiguous, exploring both sides of its suggested meaning: "It's not your thoughts that matter/You are not your thoughts" vs. "Something's going on/But it's not what you think it is." I still like that song quite a bit, but I'm not sure other people like it or "get" it. By the way, on the subject of stealing, I completely stole a chord sequence from "God Only Knows" for the bridge of "It's Not What You Think."

OK, so clichés as song titles and refrains are good: They lend context, can make your song easier to remember, can add layers of background meaning without actually having to spell it out and with a twist can be both funny and poignant. Internal clichés, within the verse lyrics themselves, can be really boring, though. Stuff like: "It hurt me so bad," "when you walked out the door," "the skies are all turned gray," "I'm so lonely now," "you were the best part of me," "baby, come back," blah blah blah. Then the lyrics become useless and meaningless. You're saying nothing that anyone could have an actual felt response to. Even if you *are* sad that your baby left you, using cliché phrases in the lyrics becomes trite and meaningless. This, I think, is the heart of what "cheesiness" is.

Almost all songs are based in extreme or semi-extreme emotional states: pain, sorrow, anger or joy. So being emotional unto itself isn't "cheesy." If it were, then nearly every song ever written would be cheesy — and maybe you could make a case for that. So it's the way you say it, and the musical setting, that decides whether you've crossed over your personal "cheese" line. Everyone has his or her own tolerance level for what we call cheese or sentimentality. But with songwriting — or any art, really — if you're not writing right up against your own personal cheese line, then you're not fully emotionally engaged. That's where your real emotional truth lives. If you hold back in fear of being cheesy, your listeners will sense that, and they'll wonder why they should bother to care if you don't even have the guts to engage. If you go over your cheese line, you can always scale it back. You can always edit. But don't pre-edit out of fear as you're writing. This is very, very, very difficult. Explore your cheese line.

I think a string of clichéd lines in the verses also makes for cheese. This is the where the "show, don't tell" rule applies. Use real things from your own experience, and use images that appeal to the senses: sight, sound, touch and occasionally taste and smell. Also, you should probably avoid rhyming words that have been rhymed a billion times, as Merritt mentions. So rhyming "love" with pretty much anything should no longer be allowed (especially "glove"), along with the classic "moon/spoon/June/tune" and "dance/romance/trance/glance" and "fire/desire/higher." Those all need to go away forever. I'm sure there are more. (Mark: nominates "on my knees/begging you please.") Maybe we should be writing a glossary of rhymes no longer permitted.

As we discussed earlier, popular music has been moving away from perfect rhymes, but you're still going to find end rhymes, and a well-rendered, unexpected end rhyme is still going to be awesome — just like a well-placed V-to-I cadence is still going to be occasionally awesome, but it will also sound very old fashioned and "corny" in a lot of cases because popular songs have been using the V-to-I cadence since before Stephen Foster. There are more II minor or IV end cadences now. Also, most big popular songs are now in minor keys, too: Beyonce, Justin Timberlake, etc., and even a lot of pop-country songs. That's been going on for a while. I think minor keys sound more "bad ass," in the words of a songwriting student. As we discussed before, lots of hip hop is in minor keys. I've tried to make myself write in minor keys because I tend to naturally go for the majors, even though what I'm writing about is often "unhappy" in general.

Pop songs of all genres have become wordier and wordier over the past 10 years or so, I've noticed. I think that's a result of hip hop, too, but in this case I don't think it's necessarily progress. The constant rapid-fire lyric with no room to breathe can be an exhausting bummer. There are times when wordiness works, though: R.E.M.'s "It's the End of the World as We Know It (And I Feel Fine)," Chuck Berry's "Maybelline" and "Johnny B. Goode" and, of course, a lot of hip hop such as Jay-Z's "99 Problems."

M   The rock wordiness thing goes back to Dylan, right? "Subterranean Homesick Blues" — that's a groundbreaking avalanche of verbiage right there (can an avalanche be groundbreaking?), and he crammed an awful lot of words into that whole *Bringing It All Back Home/Highway 61 Revisited/Blonde on Blonde* period. As we established earlier, imitate Dylan at your own peril. And, yeah, for every "It's the End of the World…" there's a Billy Joel's "We Didn't Start the Fire" or Barenaked Ladies' "One Week." Let's also not forget Reunion's 1974 novelty classic "Life Is a Rock (But the Radio Rolled Me)," which name-checks scores of musicians, songwriters, song titles, record labels, disc jockeys, musical instruments/accessories and pop-culture miscellany in three minutes of rat-a-tat patter. That one became especially popular in Chicago as the dueling top-40 stations WCFL and WLS spun customized versions that dropped the call letters into the chorus. I'm OK with those "Life Is a Rock" songs as long as they don't come around too often.

Rap, of course, is by definition wordy, its energy driven by the rapper's ability to execute verbal gymnastics with passion, clarity and unshakable rhythm. Grandmaster Flash and the Furious Five's 1982 epic "The Message," widely considered to be the first social-commentary hip hop hit about inner city struggles, sports multiple long narrative verses punctuated by a spare, deliberate chorus in which Grandmaster Flash warns, "Don't push me 'cause I'm close to the edge/I'm trying not to lose my head." So even in the same song one can approach the balance of words and music in different ways.

As I mentioned earlier, Elvis Costello and the Attractions' *Get Happy!!* is almost claustrophobic in the way it packs lyrics into almost every musical space; instrumental passages are infrequent and quick, yet his attack fits that album's emotions and energy. Then there are albums that flip the equation, such as Brian Eno's *Another Green World*, in which the words are almost haiku-like islands floating amid vast musical oceans. Some singer-songwriters will cram seven words into a spot in which someone else might draw out one syllable or simply let the music do the talking. Figuring out where and how many words to put over a passage of music is tricky business, no? An early version of the Beach Boys' "Good Vibrations" has Brian Wilson singing on the beat, "Good! Good! Good! Good vibrations, yeah!" in the same spot that ultimately became home to the Mike Love-sung chorus, "I'm pickin' up good vibrations/She's giving me excitations..." The final version, less aggressive and built more around syncopation and counterparts, is far superior.

I assume if you asked one of your classes to put lyrics and melody to a certain piece of music, you'd get vastly varying volumes of words, which would wind up in different places with different emphases in each song.

Do you have a consistent approach to how you layer words and music?

Is there always a balance to be struck between how much you want to say vs. how much room a song must have to "breathe"? Have you ever rewritten a song to give it completely different lyrics or a lot more or fewer words or words that suggest a new rhythm?

S For me, and I think for most songwriters, the music comes easier than the words. Having a phrase to begin with is really helpful. If I don't have a phrase, I let the chords suggest a melody, and then I'll write words to the rhythm and cadences of the music. I personally don't tend to think in wordy phrases and usually go the opposite direction: held notes and space. I also seem to find as I get older that I like open space in music more and more. Maybe that's a reaction to the overabundance of sensory information we're all exposed to every waking moment of every day. I feel like music can be a tonic to that; that's what I personally seem to be craving more and more and probably why I'm bugged by the increasing wordiness of popular music.

That said, I do have some pretty wordy stuff on the most recent Dolly Varden album, especially the song, "Done (Done)." That was written as a folky finger-picked storytelling song, and I turned it into an up-tempo thumping rock song. I completely changed the music and kept the words intact. I guess if I feel I have a workable lyric (the hard part, for me), I'll try to find the best musical setting for it (the easier and more fun part). Even if the lyric was derived from a musical framework, I'm OK with changing the musical setting if it casts the lyric better. I've done this often.

M   That reminds me of one of your assignments, in which you had folks write new lyrics to "This Land Is Your Land" and then write new music to those lyrics. *Voila!* — new song. (See Assignment 4, p. 134.) Now back to clichés...

One of the many ridiculous, unfulfilled ideas I've had over the years was to record an album of songs comprised only of the most clichéd, overused titles: "Lady," "Hold On," "I Love You," etc. That inability to copyright titles is one of the creative world's great loopholes, and it applies to movies, too (the spelling-bee *Spellbound* documentary bore no relation to the Hitchcock film) and some band names (there was a '60s band called Nirvana). I'm occasionally mystified when bands borrow titles and phrases strongly associated with previous songs; Jellyfish included a song called "You're My Best Friend" on an album filled with Queen sound-alikes, and the overtly Beatles-influenced Badfinger recorded original songs called "Love Me Do," "Money" and "Flying." I also was a bit stunned when Tom Petty sang about "a rebel without a clue" on "Into the Great Wide Open" when the Replacements had used that phrase on their closest thing to a hit, "I'll Be You."

That said, there are only so many word combinations out there, and sometimes you create a song around a phrase that has been employed previously. I have one song that lands on the line "Sorry, I'm already gone," but I don't want to call it "Already Gone" because of the Eagles hit, and I don't want to include "I'm" in the title, so I'll have to think of something else. Another long-unfinished song is called "The Last Resort," and guess what? That's an Eagles title too, though in this case I hadn't heard of the song before I wrote mine. (That's right, I don't own *Hotel California*.) I feel like I'd be on safer ground with "The Last Resort" than "Already Gone," but we'll see. (Memo to self: Don't write a song called "Witchy Woman.")

One song I wrote for your class has a chorus that goes, "Come, baby, come back..." That's what came out when I was writing it, and I haven't changed it; my hope was that the phrasing is odd enough to justify the variation on a cliché. I have another song I half-wrote many years ago that begins, "Don't cry, darling, don't cry, and I'll take you home." I've never finished that song in part because I fear that opening is nudging me into cheeseland, yet those are the words that popped out as I made up the song, and I have yet to shake them after many years; they fit the music's mood. Then again, "Don't cry" and "I'll take you home" probably came easily *because* they're clichés. There's also an "It'll be all right" in there — *arrgh* — and the song goes back and forth between the I and IV chords a fair amount, so I'm not exactly tilling new ground. I probably should wipe the slate clean lyrically, but part of me thinks I ought to follow your "finish your bad songs" advice and pursue the path I've laid out without so much self-consciousness and try to stay true to the song's emotions regardless of the clichés. Time to call on my song-editing skills, right? I *would* have to think of a title other than the way-overused "Don't Cry," though.

To me there's a difference between leaning on a cliché and taking ownership of a familiar phrase. "I Won't Back Down," for instance, is not an uncommon sentiment or combination of words, but it also wasn't associated with hundreds of songs before Petty made it his own. The same can be said about most of your examples. But I wouldn't want to hear a song called "A Penny Saved (Is a Penny Earned)." On Lennon's final recordings, he could sing about "Watching the Wheels" in a way that felt original while "(Just Like) Starting Over" was a bit more hackneyed yet rang true, and the posthumously released "Borrowed Time" was too much of a cliché for my taste. On a side note, I always thought he got away with one on "Woman," because (a) it's another one of those ubiquitous titles (did you know McCartney wrote a song for Peter & Gordon called "Woman" under the pseudonym Bernard Webb?), (b) what kind of enlightened soul actually addresses his wife or girlfriend as "woman"? (c) why on earth does the singer feel mixed emotions at his thoughtlessness? Moving on…

Really, it's sort of a miracle that *everything* isn't a cliché at this point. Millions of songs have been written over thousands of years using the same limited number of notes — and most covering a finite range of subjects — yet we keep trying to create something new and good. And guess what? I'm constantly hearing new, good songs, whether on the radio or in local clubs or, for that matter, your class. Songwriting is closer to alchemy than science; there's no set way to pursue it and certainly no set way to discuss it. Two other songwriters could have generated this many pages of conversation and hit on completely different points than we did here. There are at least as many ways to approach this stuff as there are note combinations.

So…what's it all about, Stevie? (Sorry.)

What's the big takeaway for someone sitting down at the keyboard or pulling out a guitar/ukelele/banjo/mandolin/kazoo/what-have-you and thinking: OK, time to create?

S   Well, I think the big takeaway is this: Learn all you can from great songs that have come before, try to internalize a sense of song form, melodic development and harmony (chords), write lyrics off the top of your head without editing as you go, and eventually, hopefully, you'll find yourself coming up with songs that you can tolerate. The second step is, of course, developing your editing "tool box" — and that includes a working knowledge of chords and keys, proficiency on a chordal instrument, an ability to hear language for its rhythm and music and the ability to be honest with yourself about when lyrics and music need re-working.

There's a lot that goes into a good song. When a great songwriter conjures a brilliant new song from "thin air," we should acknowledge the years and years of work that came before that moment. I sometimes compare it to legendary jazz saxophonist John Coltrane, who practiced for hours and hours and weeks and years running scales, learning tunes and developing his sound. Then when he made a recording or played a concert, he didn't actively think at all; he let the music come through him. Could Coltrane's deep well of stunning music have been created without those countless hours of practice? I don't think so. So apply those hours to learning all you can, and then try to forget about it when you are writing. Then get your toolbox out, and get to editing.

Songwriting is an art form that hits both the head and the heart. Music was the first form of language and has a profound effect on all of us. Which music is "good" and which is "bad" is so subjective from person to person and from culture to culture that to make any kind of absolute qualification is silliness. Some music is more challenging, and some requires a learning curve to appreciate, but does that make it better? That's a matter of opinion. One person can hear a song and have it hit them so deeply that it's life-changing, and another person can hear that same song and hate it so much that it makes them angry. People have responded to rhythm first since the beginning of time; that's in our brain stems. Rhythm will always be the first thing people react to.

The next thing would be overall timbre and the sound of a singer's voice combined with the instruments and sonic environment. Next would be melody, chords and finally words. Some people *never* get to the words. Lyrics are the least noticed part of songs, and that's what we spend the most time suffering over. There are a small percentage of people, like me, who can't abide a song with terrible lyrics. It drives me nuts, and it always has. I don't know why that is.

I think that a good lyric combined with a good rhythm, chord changes and melody is the highest, most moving and immediate form of art there is. I strive to make songs that could potentially resonate with people the way certain songs resonated with me when I was growing up.

M
Do you feel like you've succeeded? And have you ultimately gotten as much pleasure out of the songs you've written as those you've listened to?

S

Well, my answer to that would be like the often-quoted line about Chicago (the city, not band): "Don't like the weather, wait 10 minutes." Feelings of success and failure come and go like waves on a beach. Some days I feel great about my work, and other days I feel like I'm only beginning to understand what I even want to do or how I want to go about it. I don't derive much actual pleasure from writing or singing songs. That may sound weird since I've been obsessively driven to do it since I was 14 years old, and I haven't really ever taken a break. I'll try to explain.

Songwriting seems to come from a very basic, primal place, and I wouldn't be able to turn it off even if I wanted to. There's not any sense of pleasure or anything else, really. It just sort of is. I am happy when a song gets written that works and seems to contain some kind of magical potential. I am happy when I sing a song and people respond to it. Those things are fleeting, though. Because of the way human creative cycles go, I begin to doubt the songs relatively soon after they've been written. I know I'm not alone in feeling this. I think the fact that not only have I often felt this but that I'm willing to admit it is one of the reasons my songwriting classes continue be full of students.

I've read a lot of books and taken classes on songwriting, and I find the prevailing arrogant attitude of "I know how to do this, just follow my example" to be disingenuous. Sure, there are techniques that always work and crafting tools to learn, but those things alone don't make for a great song. They can make a well-crafted song. I saw on one teacher's website that they could teach you how to write a hook. I think that's crazy. A truly great hook — melodic, harmonic, rhythmic, lyric — comes from inspiration and experimentation and then gets nuanced by craft. You can't teach inspiration. You can tell a student, "Learn all you can and then forget it. Give yourself space and time to play without judgment, and write as much and as often as you can. At some point you'll write some things you'll be relatively happy with, maybe even a great song that people will sing for years to come."

So it's not about pleasure. What is it about? Why not choose to do something more practical that will actually pay the bills and provide some kind of security? There was a music business seminar at Berklee when I was there, and the speaker said basically, "If you have any choice at all about getting out of the music business, get out now. Run away. Don't look back. It's a disastrous career choice, and you will never be truly secure. If there's no other option for you, and if there's absolutely nothing else you can possibly see yourself doing with your life, then accept it and be prepared to struggle."

Music is like a religion. Or maybe more of a cult. A calling of sorts. I don't know. It's all I've ever really been interested in since I was a teenager, and it's still how I spend most of my time. There have been moments of actual pleasure — I don't want to sound too dour about all this — and I probably wouldn't change much if I could go back and start over. Certainly I'd still choose to be a musician and a songwriter. I would make different choices in the way I went about the business of music.

Your question starts with "Do you feel like you've succeeded?" The answer is, of course, not so simple. I do feel like I've written songs that I'm proud of and that people enjoy. I've played a lot of shows over

Music is like a religion. Or maybe more of a cult. A calling of sorts.

the years that are happy memories. Through singing and writing I've met many wonderful people and traveled to lots of cool places that I wouldn't have had the chance to do otherwise. I basically met my wife through music, and it has been a deep connection and anchor for the two of us for more than 25 years now. Occasionally a song hits home so deep that I can barely continue. I am still as moved by music as I was when I was 14, and I am still absolutely intrigued and interested in songwriting, and I feel that my best work is yet to come. These things I would count as "success."

In terms of the business of music, I have not fared as well. When I had the best opportunities — when I was in my 20s, and the biz was still flush with money and actively looking for new acts — I was paranoid, ignorant and hot-headed, had a sense of entitlement and wasn't prepared to risk much. Both of my bands were offered recording contracts with major labels, and both turned them down because we were advised, and I believed, that we deserved better. If I could go back, I'd sign both of those contracts now with some humility and take my chances.

It occurs to me as I get older that the people who are very successful in whatever business they choose are the ones who basically risk everything and then work their asses off. In the music biz that means letting go of any sense of security, any lasting relationships, any sense of a home or a family and getting in a van and playing show after show after show for years and years. It also means being a shameless and tireless self-promoter or finding someone who will be your shameless and tireless promoter.

There's a lot of luck involved as well. Talent is needed but not more than the other stuff and maybe actually less. It is, by definition, a selfish way to go about life. All that I've read about Steve Jobs tells me he was one of the most selfish men who ever lived. I'm not using "selfish" with the full negative connotation it usually has, but if you can separate negativity from the word and just approach it as factual — really successful people are driven solely by the focus on themselves and their work without regard to others — I think that's true.

I've never really been able to do any of that stuff to the degree needed. I have been plenty selfish at times, but I have too much self doubt, and I was never able to risk everything. I'm bad at self-promotion and never lucked upon anyone who'd work that angle for me. I craved a home, a family and security. I came from a broken home with a deeply depressed, alcoholic mother. My dad walked out on us when I was nine, and then two years later, after my mom tried to kill herself, we ended up going to live with him and moving to Idaho. It was a huge, troubled mess that's left me with a need for a real home and stability. I've always had a "day job" to pay the bills. I got married relatively young and have lived in the same house for more than 25 years. I've never really enjoyed touring all that much. The shows generally are good, and I like all the people in the band, but I hate the hours and hours of down time sitting in a van or a motel or a stinky bar. It makes me dulled out, anxious and crazy. So in these terms I am not a success in the music business.

It used to make me feel like a failure at times, but as I get older I realize that it's just the reality of who I am. I do still actively write, perform and record songs, and though my audience is relatively small, I have an audience that is interested in what I do. I am more and more able to feel that is success. We did a 10-day tour of the UK in February 2011, and I was able truly to enjoy it by letting go of expectations and feelings of success or failure and just playing the music and enjoying the sightseeing. That may sound simplistic, but to me it was revelatory.

An unexpected and wonderful thing happened in 2004 that changed my life and the way I think about success and failure. As I said, I'd been working "day jobs" to pay the bills since I left Berklee. I worked in a bookstore and a big corporate printing place, and I was the world's worst waiter. The job I had the longest was working in a record store. It was meant to be temporary until I could support myself in the music biz, but as five years turned into 10, it became more and more apparent that I had to find a more satisfying and less embarrassing way to make money. I didn't know what to do or how to go about it.

By 2004 it became a make-or-break situation. Dolly Varden was on hiatus after a very grueling year of touring, my mother had just passed away, and I was feeling really stuck and rudderless. A friend of mine was teaching guitar classes at the Old Town School of Folk Music. He liked it OK, but he said to me, "Steve, you'd be perfect there. It's all about songs: singing and playing old folk songs, Neil Young songs, Beatles songs — you know all that stuff." I'd never thought about teaching guitar and didn't know how I felt about it, but I contacted the school and asked.

The school offered me two guitar classes in the fall of 2004, and it felt good right away. In 2005 one of the songwriting teachers moved away, and they offered me his classes. Right away I loved teaching songwriting. It was really weird and unexpected. I also really loved hearing what students came up with, and I was stunned by the quality and variety of the material. All my life I'd believed the lie that only a handful of "special" people are gifted and talented enough to write and sing songs and that the very best of those people become well known. As it turns out, there are people all around all of us who are making up cool songs all the time — like you, Mark Caro! It's true! For one reason or another, most people will never hear those songs. It was a huge revelation for me.

Sometimes when I tell people I teach songwriting classes, they roll their eyes and say, "Oh, my God, how can you stand it?" I can honestly say it is a privilege and a pleasure to help people nurture their creative impulses to write songs and that a sizable percentage of the songs in my classes are very good. Occasionally the songs I hear in class are staggeringly good, and for the most part the songwriters in the classes are doing it for themselves, to enrich their own lives. Some of them self-release albums, some sing their songs at local gigs, and some of them never play their songs outside of class, ever. I would have to say that finding the Old Town School of Folk Music and discovering that I seem to have a knack for teaching music and for gently encouraging and urging people to strive to write better songs is a mid-life success that I am deeply grateful for.

It also has helped me understand that success in music isn't a "yes" or "no" thing, that there is a huge span of "success" — from the fella who sits at home writing beautiful songs for himself that no one will ever hear to Bono — and that there is much to appreciate all across that spectrum. It has also helped me understand that I fit in somewhere between that guy and Bono and that I'm basically OK with that.

OK, I'm rambling now. I told you it would be complicated. I should have just said, "Yes."

M   That's fascinating, revealing and inspiring, Steve, because it gets at the heart of what so many songwriters struggle with: Why are we doing this? You're a natural as a teacher, I suspect, because teaching gets you back to the heart of the song, and that's what you're about. You're also open-hearted and receptive, which is reflected in your classroom approach as well as your music. (Oh, and thanks for the cool songs compliment.) What your Berklee speaker said is applicable to almost any creative endeavor: Don't do it for the money. That's not to say that artists can't be commercially successful or mindful of the financial realities, but the odds are mightily against you, and if you make the business calculation intrinsic to your approach, you're likely to taint your artistic impulses. Certainly when it's just you and your guitar, thoughts about a monetary payoff aren't going to help that song come out.

Of course, I view your career differently than you do because I've been enjoying your music for more than 25 years via Stump the Host, Dolly Varden and your various offshoots. Your live performances and recordings have brought me great pleasure, and I know many other people who feel the same way. One reason for that is the joy that you convey, regardless of what you may actually be feeling at a given point.

When you're on stage, you give the impression of being completely in the moment, whether you're yelping off mic as a guitar break begins or gazing over to Diane as your vocals intertwine. Then again, you said recently in one of your classes that when you're looking at Diane while you sing, it's not because you can't contain your warm, gooey thoughts but rather that you're watching the way her mouth moves so you can sync up your harmonies. There's a reason we call this stuff *performance* — there are so many practical considerations involved in creating the magic. At the same time, I am under the impression that music transforms you, and the power of that is communicated to your audience.

It's true that your music hasn't achieved the kind of cultural penetration of, say, R.E.M. or Ryan Adams; the mega-commercial breakthrough has eluded you. But that doesn't make the music any less enjoyable — or *successful* on its own terms. "Mayfly," from the most recent Dolly Varden album, is as stunning a song as I heard that year. Will it ever break out in the manner of Adams' "Lucky Now"? Will it be appreciated well after the fact like the music of Nick Drake (though under less dreary circumstances, I would hope)? Can you control any of that? I don't know. But that song exists now, and it didn't before, and this simple point strikes me as the one that towers above all others: The song added beauty to the world.

It *lives*.

Likewise, my own drive to write or to complete songs isn't particularly results oriented. I've been making up songs or parts of songs for a few decades now, and most of them exist either in my head or as very rough demos on cassettes or digital files that I recorded solo and sloppily. If I dropped dead tomorrow, I'd hope that somebody would find these cassettes (labeled "Scratches," for future reference) or sound files and would do something with these melodies, kind of the reverse of Billy Bragg and Wilco resuscitating old Woody Guthrie lyrics. Yes, this is a completely presumptuous fantasy, but my feeling is these distinct combinations of notes and rhythms have been brought into existence and deserve someone to breathe life into them.

That someone, of course, should be me — and I *have* been making some more comprehensive demos of some of the songs, at least. I harbor no delusions regarding stardom or taking a turn in the spotlight at this point; if I were truly interested in that, I would have been motivated to do something about it at a much earlier age. What's driving me isn't ambition but the songs themselves. They're demanding my attention because I've half-created and then neglected them. Maybe this speaks to your (and Randy Newman's) earlier point about immortality, but what I want most of all is for these songs to *exist,* even if I'm ultimately the only one who cares. As long as I leave them orphaned out there, I feel like I'm guilty of some moral failing.

And as someone who still has a sense of novelty about such things, I get almost giddy hearing a song go from an idea in my head to a recording with multiple instruments and vocal parts. I find that alchemy thrilling. When I was writing for the *Boston Phoenix* after college, I probably derived more lasting pleasure from a four-track demo I recorded of a song called "Rainbow Rhinoceros" than from any of the fairly ambitious articles I wrote.

There's a quote that I've seen in various places, including a Jewish prayer book, that particularly speaks to me. It's attributed to Oliver Wendell Holmes Sr., and it goes like this:

Alas for those that never sing
But die with all their music in them

I don't want that to be me, and I'm guessing I share that sentiment with many others. The songs must find their way out, and our job is to do what we can to let them do so.

In a way the songs are writing us. Agree?

S   Oh, man, that's a perfect quote, and much of what you just said is exactly right — that we want the songs to exist — and that to ignore or orphan them seems like some kind of moral failing. Songwriting is a beautiful thing.

Assignments

STEVE   I've been teaching songwriting classes for nine years now, and I've given out a new writing assignment nearly every week. That makes more than 300 of 'em.

Some assignments really help inspire people to come up with unexpectedly wonderful songs. Some don't work so well. I never know which ones will yield the best results. Songwriting remains mysterious. Assignments work differently for different people, and you never know which will inspire you.

A big motivating factor in the weekly classes is the deadline. Students are expected to come in each week with a new song — or at least a new song started. Without the classroom structure, you will have to find ways to set your own deadlines. Perhaps schedule meet-ups with other songwriters, or make plans to play a new song live the next time you perform, or just decide that exactly a week from when you read the assignment, you will have finished a song.

The assignments are intended to be a creative spark, but I always say that it's better to write the song that wants to be written than to try to adhere strictly to the assignment's "rules." So if your imagination pulls away from the assignment, that's fine. The goal always is to write a new song.

Each assignment primarily addresses one of the five key aspects of songwriting: Form, Lyrics, Harmony (chords), Melody, Rhythm.

I often will include some other secondary aspects to keep the assignment fun and interesting. In addition, I usually give one "style" assignment where the goal is to try to match the work of a certain classic artist or songwriter.

My goal as a teacher is to have students become more open to their own creativity. Songwriting, for me, is a magical thing. I don't claim to know exactly where the inspirations for songs come from, and, frankly, I don't want to know. I believe that we all have the ability to tap into the creative forces within and without us. The assignments are meant to offer possible ways to open creative doors.

I also stress the importance of "post-inspiration" editing and crafting. That's where you take out all of your "tools" — knowledge of music theory and song form, instrumental ability, facility with language and rhyming, etc. — and rework your song until it's as good as it can be.

My classes are not about writing "hit" songs. Plenty of other books are available that claim they can help you do that. These assignments are meant to help you to find your creative voice and to generate a body of work. If you put your whole self into them, you just might end up liking a few of your songs!

Song Form

Terms: The meanings of these terms for song form may vary depending on who's talking and the style of music being described. For instance, the chorus in songs written for Broadway in the 1930s is different from the chorus in a 1960s pop song. In Broadway terminology the chorus was essentially the heart of the song after the preamble, which typically was called the verse. We will be using terms most commonly associated with contemporary popular music.

Verse: This is the part that gives you details in the lyrics and usually sets the song's mood, rhythm and musical palette. If there's a story, the verses move it along. If the song is a statement, the verses provide evidence. The verse can tell you the who, what, where, when, how and maybe the why of the song. Each verse is traditionally musically identical — same chords and melody — while the words are different for each one.

Refrain: For our purposes a refrain is a line or phrase, often the song's title, that begins or ends each verse. It is the same each time. It is usually what the song is *about*. Figures of speech, colloquialisms, cliché phrases and word play based on common phrases are often used as refrains. Think "The Times They Are a-Changin' " (final line of each verse) or "Hey Jude" (first line of each verse).

Chorus: This is a stand-alone section that repeats during the song and, musically, should be the highlight through melodic, harmonic and rhythmic emphasis. It is meant to be remembered. Lyrically it is often a summary or "thesis statement" for the song and usually contains the title. Each chorus in a song is traditionally musically and lyrically identical. If you're going to sing along with a part of a song, it's likely to be the chorus. (Think "Yellow Submarine" or "We Are the Champions.") Can a song have both a refrain and a chorus? Yes, it can. Is a refrain the same as a chorus? No, it is not. A chorus stands alone musically and lyrically while a refrain is musically and lyrically embedded into each verse. Then you get clever folks such as the Beatles, whose "Paperback Writer" writes its own rules; it appears to have a separate chorus and refrain that both consist solely of the title phrase. (Chorus: the overlapping "Paperback writer" part that opens the song. Refrain: the verse-ending "...to be a paperback writer/ *Paperback writer!*")

Bridge: This is a separate section that most often occurs more than halfway through a song, usually after two verse/refrains or two verse/choruses. It is musically and lyrically new and can be viewed as a palate cleanser for the song, something to offer contrast. Changes in key can work well at the bridge. You *do not need* a bridge, though, so don't feel obligated to write one. Many, many fine songs are simple verse-refrain or verse-chorus songs with no bridge, but it is a skill worth exploring.

Pre-chorus: This "ramp" into the chorus is a new section musically and lyrically that's not part of the verse but works to set up the chorus. The "The scars of your love…" section of Adele's "Rolling in the Deep," the "But oh, how it feels so real…" part of Elton John's "Tiny Dancer" and the operatic buildup of Queen's "We Are the Champions" are classic pre-choruses.

Intro: An opening passage that sets up a song's mood or tone. It can be anything from the chords of the verse or chorus (the Eagles' "Hotel California," which uses the verse chords) to a separate, composed piece of music (the Beach Boys' "California Girls" and "Wouldn't It Be Nice").

Coda: A composed ending to a song, more involved than a simple outro. Sometimes a coda is just a couple of chords or a slightly altered melody at the end of the song. Some famous codas are the "Na na na…" part of "Hey Jude" and the extended instrumental passage that ends Derek and the Dominoes' "Layla."

Tag: This form of ending involves taking a piece of the hook and repeating it two, three or more times, either to be faded out (as in Johnny Nash's "I Can See Clearly Now," the Everly Brothers' "Cathy's Clown" or the Beach Boys' "God Only Knows," the last featuring those sublimely overlapping harmonies) or to come to a cold stop (the Knack's "My Sharona").

Here are examples of how some common song forms work, though keep in mind that you have leeway in playing with these structures and should serve the song's needs first:

Verse

Verse, verse, verse — the most basic structure, common in folk songs and storytelling songs. This form goes back hundreds of years; this is how troubadours would sing their stories.

Verse 1
Verse 2
Verse 3

Examples: "California Stars," Wilco/Woody Guthrie; the traditional English-Scottish folk song "Barbara Allen"; "Pineloa," Lucinda Williams; "All Along the Watchtower," Bob Dylan.

12-Bar Blues

A variation on Verse form in which each 12-bar verse most often has this structure:

Line 1
Repeat line 1 over IV chord
New line with a harmonic "turnaround" and usually a rhyme

Examples: "Bright Lights, Big City," Jimmy Reed; "She Belongs To Me," Bob Dylan; "Blue Car," Greg Brown; "Saskatchewan to Chicago," Dolly Varden; "Got My Mojo Working," popularized by Muddy Waters though written by Preston Foster.

Verse with Refrain

Each verse begins or ends with the same phrase, which is attached to the verse lyrically and musically. Often the rhyme structure is set up to connect the refrain to each verse.

Verse 1 + refrain
Verse 2 + refrain
Verse 3 + refrain

Examples: "Funny How Time Slips Away," Willie Nelson; "The Sound of Silence," Simon & Garfunkel; "The Times They Are a-Changin'," Bob Dylan.

Verse/Chorus

Many pop and folk songs have this structure, often with two or three verses and perhaps an instrumental break after the second chorus, most often using the verse chords.

Verse 1
Chorus
Verse 2
Chorus
(musical break)
Verse 3
Chorus

Examples: "Purple Rain," Prince; "You've Got To Hide Your Love Away," the Beatles; "American Pie," Don McLean; "Be My Baby," the Ronettes.

Verse with Refrain + Bridge (AABA form)

The classic popular pre-rock 'n' roll song form found in thousands of songs: two verses with a common refrain as the first or last line of each; a bridge that goes somewhere new musically, lyrically or both; and one more verse with refrain. It's a beautiful form to get to know.

Verse 1 + refrain
Verse 2 + refrain
Bridge
Verse 3 + refrain

Examples: "Don't Get Around Much Anymore," Duke Ellington; "Georgia On My Mind," Hoagy Carmichael; "Will You Still Love Me Tomorrow," Gerry Goffin and Carole King (popularized by the Shirelles).

Sometimes called AABABA, this form is directly derived from the classic AABA form above. John, Paul and George used this song form for many of their best-loved songs.

Verse 1 + refrain
Verse 2 + refrain
Bridge
Verse 3 + refrain
Repeat Bridge
Repeat Verse 3 or 1

Examples: "We Can Work It Out," "Yesterday," "You Won't See Me," "I Will."

Verse/Chorus with Bridge

Here we add a bridge between the second chorus and third verse for a musical palate cleanser and lyrical departure. Sometimes the lyrics of the bridge take a step back for a "big picture" view of the song; sometimes they get more intimate. Often the bridge will use new chords and melody notes not heard in the verses or chorus.

Verse 1
Chorus
Verse 2
Chorus
Bridge
Verse 3
Chorus

Examples: "I Want It That Way," Backstreet Boys; "Thriller," Michael Jackson; "Here Comes The Sun," the Beatles; "Accidents Will Happen," Elvis Costello.

FORM VARIATIONS

Those are the main basic song forms and how they are arranged. Here are some common variations:

Double Verse Before Chorus

A more complex song form that allows for more storytelling development before the chorus. Often this form is arranged so that the first verse is just the vocalist with spare accompaniment, with a full band coming in at the top of the second verse.

Verse 1
Verse 2
Chorus
Verse 3
Chorus
Bridge (optional)
Verse 3 and/or Chorus

Examples: "Bad Day," Daniel Powter; "Free Falling," Tom Petty; "I've Just Seen a Face," the Beatles.

Pre-Chorus

As described above the pre-chorus is a ramp into each chorus. Often it ends in the dominant (V) chord of the song's key, with the chorus starting on the tonic (the I chord). So if the song is in C major, it might sound like this:

Pre-chorus: Dm Em F G
Chorus: C F Am F

Verse 1
Pre-Chorus
Chorus
Verse 2
Pre-Chorus
Chorus
Bridge (optional)
Verse 3 (optional)
Pre-Chorus
Chorus

Examples: "Shake It Off,' Taylor Swift' "Royals," Lorde; "Time of the Season," the Zombies; "Fireworks," Katy Perry; "Good Lovin'," the Rascals; "Senses Working Overtime," XTC.

A great way to start a pop song, but it does present some problems mid-song if you're not careful, because the chorus could grow tiresome if repeated too often.

Chorus
Verse 1
Chorus
Verse 2
Chorus or Bridge
Verse 3
Chorus

Examples: "She Loves You," the Beatles; "This Land Is Your Land," Woody Guthrie; "I Shot the Sheriff," Bob Marley; "You Give Love a Bad Name," Bon Jovi; and, we're duty-bound to note, "We Built This City," Starship.

Major

Tonic			Sub-dominant	Dominant	Relative Minor		Common Non-Diatonic Chords		
I	ii	iii	IV	V	vi	vii	bVII	IImajor	ivm
C	Dm	Em	F	G	Am	B°	Bb	D	Fm
G	Am	Bm	C	D	Em	F#°	F	A	Cm
D	Em	F#m	G	A	Bm	C#°	C	E	Gm
A	Bm	C#m	D	E	F#m	G#°	G	B	Dm
E	F#m	G#m	A	B	C#m	D#°	D	F#	Am
B	C#m	D#m	E	F#	G#m	A#°	A	C#	Em
F#/Gb	Abm	Bbm	Cb	Db	Ebm	F°	E	G#	Bm
Db	Ebm	Fm	Gb	Ab	Bbm	C°	B	Eb	Gb
Ab	Bbm	Cm	Db	Eb	Fm	G°	Gb	Bb	Eb
Eb	Fm	Gm	Ab	Bb	Cm	D°	Db	F	Abm
Bb	Cm	Dm	Eb	F	Gm	A°	Ab	C	Ebm
F	Gm	Am	Bb	C	Dm	E°	Eb	G	Bbm

° = diminished

Minor

i	ii	III	iv	V	VI	VII
Am	B°	C	Dm	E	F	G
Em	F#°	G	Am	B	C	D
Bm	C#°	D	Em	F#	G	A
F#m	G#°	A	Bm	C#	D	E
C#m	D#°	E	F#m	G#	A	B
G#m	A#°	B	C#m	D#	E	F#
Ebm	F°	Gb	Abm	Bb	Cb	Db
Bbm	C°	Db	Ebm	F	Gb	Ab
Fm	G°	Ab	Bbm	C	Db	Eb
Cm	D°	Eb	Fm	G	Ab	Bb
Gm	A°	Bb	Cm	D	Eb	F
Dm	E°	F	Gm	A	Bb	C

Based on harmonic minor

THE LINE OF 4THS

E→A→D→G→C→F→Bb→Eb→Ab/G#→Db/C#→F#→B→E

Root motion in 4ths is a very powerful tool for composing chord progressions. What's root motion? The root is the letter that your chord is named for, so for any A chord — A, Am, A7, Am7(b5), A diminished, etc. — the root is A. The most common version of this is the V-to-I (that is, 5-to-1) cadence in a major key. For example, in the key of C, the V chord, G, has a very strong pull to go to the I chord, C.

This is the basic foundation of all Western music. Drama, storytelling...it all comes down to the V-to-I cadence. See how the G on the line comes just before the C? The gravitational pull of the V-to-I cadence pushes left to right on the line. Each root resolves into the next root on the line. So, here's the deal: The line is all about creating V-to-I cadences anywhere, anytime.

Every chord can have its own personal V chord, regardless of key. Make the V chord into a dominant 7th chord and the intensity is raised. (i.e. G7 instead of G). This is a good way to venture outside of a key and then find your way back. Say you have a chord progression in the key of C that you'd like to add some color and texture to...

C   Am   C   Am   Dm   G

Now, let's add some chords from the line and see how that sounds:

C   Am   C   E → Am   Dm   D7 → G

A lot of music from the 1920s and '30s (and before) uses dominant chords cycling in 4ths. Here's "Salty Dog Blues":

G   E7 → A7 → D7 → G over and over again

Start on G, go back 3 spaces on the line and then let nature take its course. Ray Davies of the Kinks uses this type of chord progression often. Have a look at "Sunny Afternoon" sometime.

A very common usage is what is often called the "V of V," or the dominant of the dominant, what I sometimes call the "major II" chord. In C it would be a D or D7; in G it would be an A or A7. This shows up everywhere: Buddy Holly, Hank Williams, the Rolling Stones, Paul Simon, often in the bridge. A clear example of this is in the song "Your Cheatin' Heart," by Hank Williams, Sr. As he sings the phrase "You'll toss around," on the word "around," the song goes to the "V of V" chord and then follows to the actual V chord on the word "name." This will be a familiar sound, and you should try to learn to identify it. It also appears just as Mick Jagger sings the word "upstairs" in the first verse of the Rolling Stones' "Honky Tonk Woman."

The chords don't have to be major or dominant, either. Root motion in 4ths is common and satisfying enough on its own that we hear the cadence even if it's not overt. So here's a progression bursting with root motion in 4ths, in the key of G:

G   B7→Em→A   Am7→D→G   Gm→C→F→Bb   A7   Am→D   D7→ G

The B7, A, Gm, F, Bb, and A7 chords are from outside the key, giving you new harmonic richness and melodic options. The B7 adds a D# melody note, the A adds a C#, the Gm adds a Bb, etc. If you can weave these notes into your melody, then you'll really be on to something!

Now that you're aware of root motion in 4ths, you will start to notice it everywhere.

And you can use it to write a song. (See Assignment 14, p. 175.)

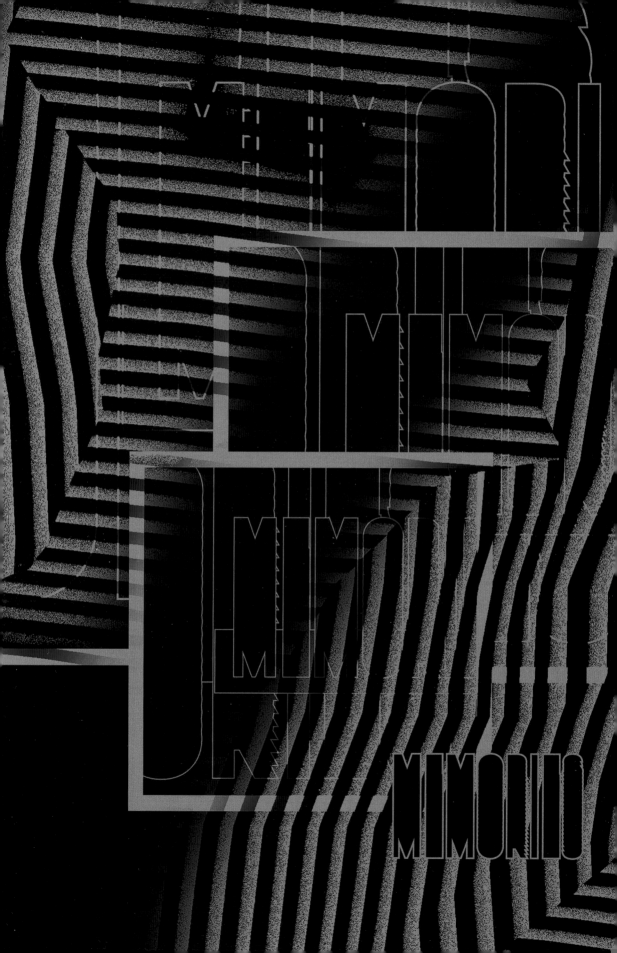

Photographs, Memories and Form

You're going to write a song that springs from an emotional memory

Find a quiet place where you can be alone, and no one can hear you, and you won't be bothered for at least 30 minutes. Turn off your phone and the Internet. Find some old photographs: actual printed photos or digital photos on your computer. It is best if they are photos from your life — of family, friends, trips taken, places you've lived, anything that has a personal connection. Look through them and pay attention to how you are feeling.

When you land on a photo that gives you an emotional reaction — joy, sadness, anger, longing, any feeling that resonates inside you — begin to write words. Describe the scene in the photo using your senses: sight, sound, touch and maybe taste and smell depending on the situation. This is how we best communicate, by appealing to the senses. Write about what you are feeling, too. Try to get to the heart of the emotional reaction.

If you land on a specific memory from the past, try to remember all you can about it. Try to put yourself back into that time and place. Be specific. Our memories are filled with rich stories that are relatable and compelling. We all love stories, and we all have similar memories of love, joy, loss and sadness. If your story is true, it will most likely be compelling to others. Specific details and images work better than general thoughts. You may think that no one will be able to relate to what you're saying if you use details only you will recognize, but I have found that is absolutely not true. The more specific and real your images are, the more people will be moved by them.

Soon into the process, get out your instrument of choice and begin playing chords in any key. Use the chords and keys chart (p. 142) to help you if you're not sure. Find chords that seem to match the feeling the photo gives you. Begin singing lines from what you've written over the chords you've chosen. Let your imagination go, and sing gibberish words if necessary. Don't worry that the chords or words are "wrong" or that they don't make literal sense. There is no "wrong" at this point.

Continue exploring this combination of chords, words and melody. When you land on something you like, repeat it. Repeat it a lot, and let it pull you deeper into the song.

Chances are the part you are repeating is the refrain or the chorus. How long is it? If it is a single line, it is probably a refrain that will be attached to a verse. If it is a longer section, it is probably a chorus.

Put some of the sensory words together to form a three- or four-line section. We'll call that Verse 1. Don't worry about rhyming just yet.

Insert the repeated part now. We'll call that Refrain or Chorus 1.

For the second verse, let your imagination go where it wants to go. Don't worry about making sense. Improvise words using the same melody and chords you used in Verse 1. Songs tend to let you know where they want to go if you are willing to listen. Try. When you come up with something tolerable, call that Verse 2.

Put the Refrain or Chorus down after that, and guess what? You've written a song!

Make a quick memo recording of the song, and write down the lyrics and chords. Then do something else for a while, maybe even a day or two. Come back to it after you've cleared your head. It will sound different than you remember. Don't get discouraged. Get to work.

Be playful and open-minded. See whether you can move any of the lines around for a better impact. Or maybe come up with a bridge if inspiration strikes. To do that, try to start with a chord you haven't used in the song yet. Begin the melody in a different range. Try using a key word from the refrain/chorus to venture into a new thought.

What about rhyming? Do you like songs that rhyme? Rhyming can be a very useful tool, but forced rhymes can be distracting. Don't let the rhymes dictate the lyric. Keep the lyric true to your idea. See whether you can make any end-of-line rhymes without changing the meaning. There are many good rhyming websites; do a search, and you'll find 'em.

After you've reworked your song a few times, play it for someone you trust.

And feel good that you just added a song to the universe.

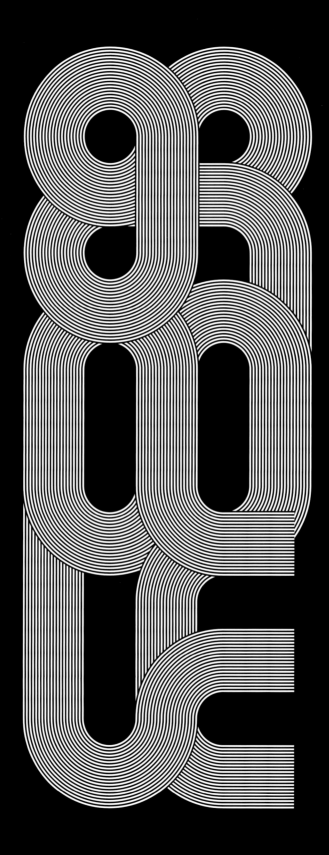

Rhythm, Duration, Space and Groove

We're going to get down to basics and anchor a song with a groove

What's the very first thing most people notice when they listen to a new song? The words? Nope. The chords? Nope. The melody? Nope. It's the groove, the feel.

What's the last thing many of us singer/songwriters think about? The groove.

Rhythm is processed by the most primitive parts of our brains, and our very selves are kept alive by rhythm: our heartbeat and breathing. Many important activities involve rhythmic regularity, including writing, walking, exercising, eating, what have you.

So for this assignment we're going to get down to basics and anchor a song with a groove. Start with a rhythm; either imagine one that you find compelling or listen to some of your favorite records and "borrow" a groove. Don't worry; there's a long-standing, time-honored tradition of borrowing grooves in songwriting. Consider what we call the Bo Diddley beat (*bump-bum-bum-bi-DAH-dum*). Bo Diddley didn't invent it — it actually has roots in African, Latin and country music — but he sure used it well, and so have many others.

Also, if you want to get legalistic, copyright protection applies to songs' melodies but not rhythms, so the groove field is wide open.

Find a groove you like and start from there. Try singing some stuff — either actual or nonsense words — that fit the groove. Sing a single phrase over and over, experimenting with where you accent the groove. For example, say your phrase is:

My heart, my heart is beating like a tom tom

That's 11 syllables, so there are 11 possible emphasis points.

__My__ heart my heart is beating like a tom tom
My __heart__ my heart is beating like a tom tom

Etc.

And/or multiple sets of emphasis:
My __heart__, my __heart__, is __beat__ing like a __tom__ tom
__My__ heart, my __heart__, is beating __like__ a tom __tom__

Lots and lots of options. Have fun with this process.

Once you've found your groove and some phrases you like, try mixing up the activity and durations of the other aspects of your song. Words, chords and melody all have rhythmic aspects. Try using a lot of words in the verse over just two or three chords that last at least two measures each. Then for the chorus, try fewer words with space between phrases while the chord activity increases, with one changing each measure or even two chords per measure. Here's an example of what I'm talking about using some nonsense words:

G   G
Ol Mister Gurdy is a heck of a loon

C   C
Similar in retrospect and half off the crown

G   G
The diligent Miss Corduroy cannot contain her bath

      C   C
And the cousins in the corner have resigned on her behalf

Chorus

  |Bm   Am G   F |D   C   F   D | G | G |
My heart   my   heart is   beating like a tom tom

Get it? That's what you're going to do.

Recap

1   Find a groove you like either from your imagination or by borrowing from one of your favorite songs.

2   Improvise phrases, sounds and nonsense words to the rhythm until you land on something you like. When you do, play around with where the words are emphasized and how they interact with the rhythm.

3   Write wordy verses with few chords.

4.   Write a chorus that has fewer words and more active chords.

Aim for two verses and two choruses, and then you'll have a song. See you on the dance floor.

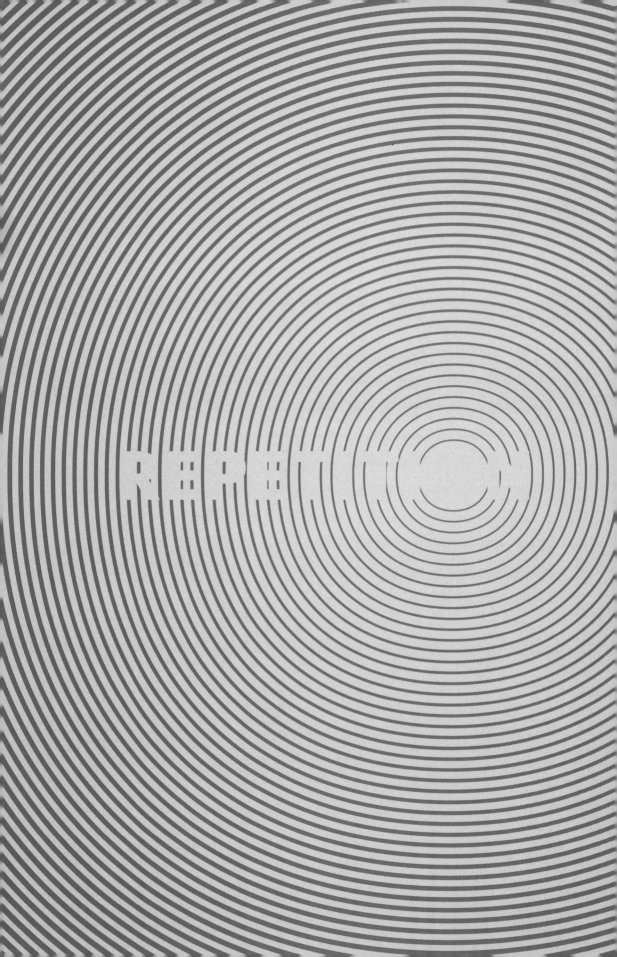

Repetition and Short Phrases

This assignment will force you to repeat lyrics, syllable counts and rhymes

Repetition is a key element in songwriting. As a writer your basic compositional decisions are based on what patterns you create and whether you'll give your listener the expected repeated pattern or something new and unexpected. A good, engaging composition will deliver both: recognizable lyric, melodic, harmonic and rhythmic patterns along with unexpected deviations from those patterns. If your song is too repetitious, it can become boring, and if it has too many surprises, it can become too difficult to follow.

The degree to which you repeat patterns or add surprises is a matter of personal taste and musical style and is subject to each listener's preferences. In general, though, I find in my classes that people don't repeat elements enough. They feel that repeating is somehow lazy or even cheating, so in trying to write "better" songs, they offer too much variation.

This assignment will force you to repeat lyrics, syllable counts and rhymes. This will create a lyric that has a built-in musical rhythm. This is certainly a "crafty" way to write, and it may feel a bit forced to you. But it is worthwhile to build up your song-crafting muscles, so do it even if it feels forced. Songwriting, like all art, is a combination of inspiration and craft.

EACH VERSE IS SIX LINES LONG

LINE 1	The *last* word(s) of line 1 will *begin* line 2. This line is six syllables or fewer.
LINE 2	The *last* word(s) of line 2 will *begin* line 3. This line is six syllables or fewer.
LINE 3	This line will end this three-line (1, 2 and 3) compound phrase. Syllable count is open — whatever works for you. Keep in mind that the word that ends this line will rhyme with the word that ends line 6.
LINE 4	The *last* word(s) of line 4 will *begin* line 5. This line has the same syllable count as line 1.
LINE 5	The *last* word(s) of line 5 will *begin* line 6. This line has the same syllable count as line 2.
LINE 6	The *last* word of this line will rhyme with the *last* word of line 3. Syllable count is open, but try to make is within one or two syllables of line 3. This line ends this three-line (4, 5 and 6) compound phrase.

EXAMPLE

LINE 1	This is a song (4 SYLLABLES)
LINE 2	A song about lines (5) (*slight rules deviation by adding "a"*)
LINE 3	Lines that will drive you to madness (8)
LINE 4	You were so young (4)
LINE 5	So young and unkind (5) (see line 2)
LINE 6	Kindness was foreign to sadness (8)

This is your verse structure. Write *three* verses of lyrics, and then write music to them. Then write an alternate section to balance it out. How that part goes is completely up to you. Maybe it will be a chorus. Maybe it will be a bridge. See what feels right.

Verse 1

Verse 2

Alternate section

Verse 3

Alternate section

Repeat Verse 1

Ending (up to you)

A note on rhyming: The English language is moving beyond exact rhymes for use in popular songs. They're often thought to sound "dated." This doesn't mean you're off the hook and shouldn't try. A great exact rhyme is a beautiful thing but harder and harder to come by. Look for close rhymes; even just a common vowel sound or common combination of consonants can work. Something like "wait" can match up with "can't" or "bite" under certain circum-stances. If you get stuck, try a rhyming dictionary website, but don't use this right away — only if you get stuck.

The music part is entirely up to you!

Enjoy.

SONGWRITING

Writing From a Title or Phrase

A good line is songwriting gold, and now you're going to write a song around one

You should always keep a notebook or memo recorder handy to write down lines as they occur to you or as you overhear them in conversation. Clichés and colloquialisms make great song titles, as do playful variations on commonly known phrases and unique and memorable groupings of words.

Here's the deal with clichés: They are great for titles and great to use in a song if the context and meaning of the cliché adds to your lyric. They are not so great if you are using them to fill space in a lyric or to describe something in a nondescript, generalized way. Use real, specific imagery from your own imagination and experience for details whenever possible.

Examples of songs written to a phrase:

"Funny How Time Slips Away," Willie Nelson

"Wild Horses," The Rolling Stones

"Born Under A Bad Sign," Albert King

"That'll Be The Day," Buddy Holly

"Crazy Little Thing Called Love," Queen

"Hey, Good Lookin'," Hank Williams

"The Times They Are A-Changin'," Bob Dylan

"Heart of Gold," Neil Young

"A Case Of You," Joni Mitchell

"One Fine Day," Gerry Goffin/Carole King (the Chiffons)

With this in mind, here is a list of lines, culled from many different sources, to use in a song. Choose one of these or search clichés and aphorisms online.

"4,000 weeks" (average life span of humans)

"Alphabet of trees"

"Standing on the corner of bitter and fine"

"The comfort of kindness"

"Where I'm likely to find it"

"No news is good news"

"Good things come to those who wait"

"I'm ready for anything"

"Kill them with kindness"

Use one of these lines as your *refrain*. It can be the first line of each verse or the last line.

Sing the line a cappella and listen for its built in rhythm and musicality. That can set the "feel" and pace for your song. Choose chords that match the phrase's sentiment.

Use either the A A A verse form or the A A B A form, where the B section is a bridge that goes to a new place harmonically. For example if your verses are in the key of G major — using any of the chords in the key of G: G, Am, Bm, C, D and Em — try going to the relative minor key (E minor) for the bridge, using the chords Em, G, Am, B7, C and D.

If you choose to have the refrain end each verse, you'll want to set it up with a rhyme. For example, here's a four-line verse ending with refrain:

Line 1	
Line 2	ends with a word that rhymes with "fine" (i.e. "wine")
Line 3	
Line 4	*Standing on the corner of bitter and fine*

Learning to write songs around a great line is very useful and will open you up to the idea that not all songs need a chorus. Many of my students have found this idea to be revelatory.

Melody

Melody is a mystery, and in this assignment we're going to explore how to find one as the basis of a song

We can mathematically break down great melodies and analyze their intervals and motifs to try to answer to the elusive question, "What makes a good melody?" but we never reach a satisfying conclusion. Most great melody writers whom I've studied speak of a spiritual component to composing melodies. They feel they are in contact with something bigger than themselves and are receiving rather than forging something from nothing. This idea may or may not appeal to you.

If the spiritual idea of music being a magical force bigger and deeper than we can even comprehend appeals to you, then go with that. If it doesn't work for you, then you could think in terms of being in dialogue with your own subconscious mind's collection of every melody you've ever heard, including bird songs, violin concertos, television advertisements and any other music you've loved or despised. Either way, you want to work toward tapping into the unknown.

I think melodies are part of our very being, linked and bound to our humanity and our DNA, and they connect us with nature and to each other. We are meant to sing, and we are meant to create melodies. The process of uncovering and discovering melodies can come very naturally to some and be very difficult and frustrating for others. Once again we may be faced with being blocked by our own internal and external litany of judgments.

At early ages we are encouraged to sing and to be playful with music, but at some point during puberty, cultural pressures begin to tell us that only famous "singers" should be singing. It is acceptable to learn to play an instrument and certainly to write words, but singing is often frowned upon as we get older. I think this is where the difficulty and blocking come from in terms of composing melodies.

Melody begins with the voice. You can sit at a piano and compose a beautiful melody, of course, but the best melodies begin with the voice and are meant to be sung. For this reason I encourage you to sing and to sing often. Let your voice explore and be playful, and don't be judgmental. If what you sing sounds like a familiar melody, great! If it sounds boring, great! If your voice can't hit all the notes, great! There is no wrong.

Sing with chords and a cappella. Sing to just a drum loop or rhythmic pattern. Sing a phrase over and over again in different parts of your voice. As you do this, you will find certain combinations of notes feel better than others. Certain vowel sounds resonate more than others — or they resonate in different places in your body. Certain intervals and note combinations will pull up emotions. Isn't that awesome? Yes. Yes, it is.

Don't worry about whether or why it's "good" or "bad." This is difficult. When you come upon a melody that you like, make a quick recording of it. Don't assume you will remember it. You usually won't. You *must* record it or, if you have the ability, write it down. Melody is elusive and shy. The more you sing, the more likely it is that a lasting melody will emerge. But it will disappear quickly, so you must make a fixed version of any melody you like.

Here are some exercises and concrete melodic techniques to try in combination with this "free" singing:

1. SING SCALES

Do Re Mi Fa Sol La Ti Do. Up and down and back again. Sing parts of scales. What parts do you like? Jump around a bit. *Do Mi, Re Fa, Do*. Notice the half steps: between notes 3 and 4 (*Mi* and *Fa*, in the key of C, would be E and F) and notes 7 and 8 (*Ti* and *Do*, in C, would be B and C.)

2. DEVELOP MOTIFS

Motifs are repeating melodic phrases. You can have exact motifs where you repeat the same notes in the same rhythm. You can have note-based motifs where you repeat the same notes but in differing rhythms. You can have interval-based motifs where the melodic shape is repeated. You can have rhythmic motifs where just the rhythmic component is repeated, but the notes change. You can use combinations of all of the above. So try them all.

Exact Motif: Sing a 5-note phrase, and then sing it again exactly the same way. Sing it again. And again.

Note-based motif: Sing a 5-note phrase. Now sing the same notes but elongate some of the notes and shorten others. Keep doing that by playing with the durations of the notes. Use the same notes each time.

Interval-based motif: Sing a 5-note phrase. Notice the shape. Where does it go up? Where does it go down? Where does it stay the same? Sing another phrase that matches the shape exactly but uses different notes. Classic example: Beethoven's Symphony No. 5. Listen to it for inspiration. It is a motif bonanza.

Rhythm-based motif: Just the rhythm is repeated, and the notes change.

3. INCORPORATE VARIATION AND RANGE

Our brains love repetition. Let me repeat that: Our brains love repetition. We love patterns and making sense of seemingly random information. We also love new things. A great melody will offer both repetition and contrast to keep a listener engaged. So once you've developed a motif that you like, repeat it for a while. Just before it becomes boring (this is a subjective moment), offer a new, contrasting melodic idea that is derived from either a different part of the scale (higher or lower) and/or a noticeably different rhythmic place. Pivot back and forth between the two ideas, keeping Motif 1 as the principle idea and the variation occurring as a break. The AABA form works beautifully for this:

A	Motif is stated.
A	Motif is repeated.
B	New melodic idea is presented.
A	Original motif is re-stated.
	There's a verse, or part of a verse.

4. ADD CHORDS

You will find that melodies can be colored in lots of different ways depending on the "setting" in which you place them. That's what chords do; they color and emphasize different aspects of melodies. Try different chords with your melody and see what happens. Sometimes it's nice to repeat a motif over and over while underpinning it with varying chords. Try it.

So your assignment is to write a great melody. Use the techniques above. Use repetition. Don't present too many melodic motifs. Find a strong one and repeat it, using a contrasting section to make it shine.

Be playful. Don't judge.

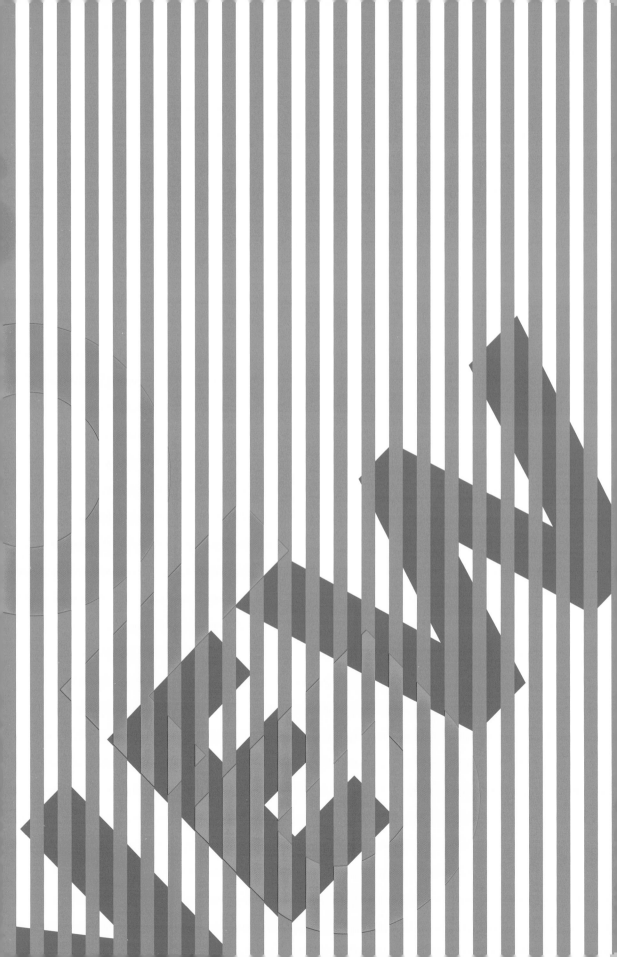

Rewrite the Words, Rewrite the Melody

You're going to write new lyrics to an old song and then write new music to your new lyrics

This one is kind of sneaky, but it has yielded some very good songs in my classes over the years. Here's the deal: You're going to write new lyrics to an old song and then write new music to your new lyrics. The old song preferably is one with a steady meter. Something like "Amazing Grace" would work or "The House of the Rising Sun," "500 Miles" or maybe even "Take Me Out to the Ballgame." I've had songwriters rework Woody Guthrie's "This Land Is Your Land." Try to use the exact cadence and syllable count.

This land is your land (5)
This land is my land (5)
From California (5)
To the New York island (6)

...

One of my students, Ross Freedman, came up with a song called "You Catch The Light" that goes like this:

Tonight there's moonshine (5)
Diffuse and yellow (5)
Ignites a dim sky (5)
Like there's a pinhole (5)
That someone poked and (5)
Released a soft night's glow (6)
You catch the light so perfectly (8)

As you can see, this song doesn't exactly repeat the syllable counts of "This Land," but you could sing these lyrics to that tune. Then again, you're not keeping that tune.

Once you have a full lyric (a few verses and maybe a chorus), the trick is to set this lyric to a new melody and chord pattern that is completely different from the Woody Guthrie tune or whichever song you have chosen. I think you'll find that this is not as hard as it seems, especially if you use a different "feel" (3/4, 6/8, altered pace, etc.). Ross used a slow, steady 16th-note-based rhythm.

New words, new music, and — voila! — you've got a new song.

Touch-tone a Song

Your phone number is the basis for your melody

NUMBER	NOTE	I.E.: IN C MAJOR
1	do	C
2	re	D
3	mi	E
4	fa	F
5	so	G
6	la	A
7	ti	B
8	do	C (octave above 1)
9	re (8va)	D (octave above 2)
0	repeat previous note	

(555) 867-5309 would be: GGG CAB GEED
You then take those notes in that order and play around with note durations and chords to come up with a melody.

Chords: G   Em   C   Em   C   G
Melody notes: G G G   C A B   G E E D

There I've composed eight measures of melody and chords using the phone number to choose the notes.

So do something like that. Feel free, once you've established this main motif using the phone number, to embellish and compose using your imagination.

Good luck.

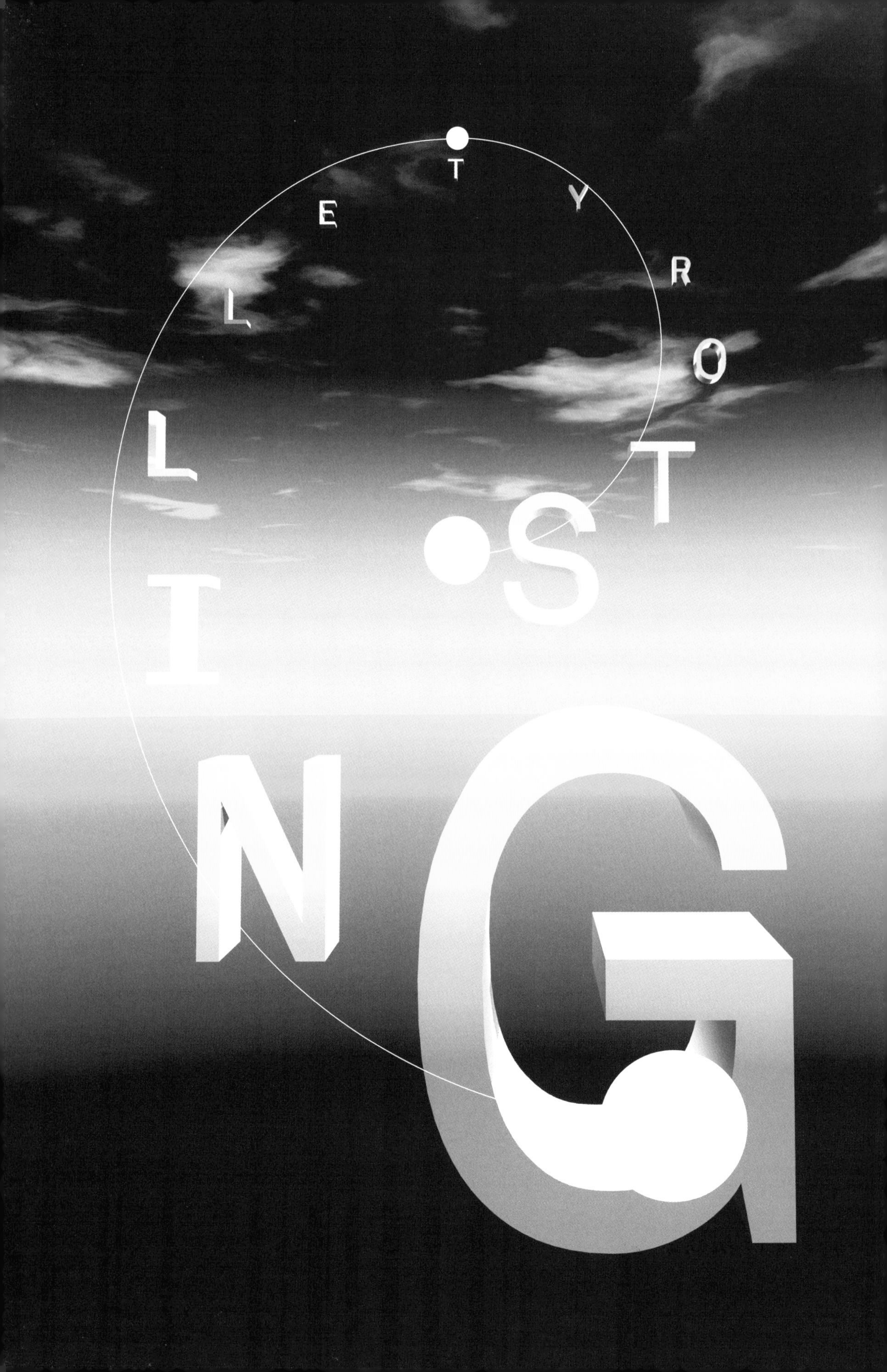
STORYTELLING

Storytelling

You are going to write a song that centers around storytelling

Since the beginning of time, people have loved storytelling. Storytelling and singing go way, way back. Epic Greek poems, such as *The Odyssey*, originally were sung. I have found that listeners find detailed storytelling to be engaging and moving even if it isn't clear what the exact storyline is. Sometimes just the suggestion of a story is all that is needed. People are curious and interested in characters and other people's lives.

You are going to write a song that centers around storytelling. It can be fictional or true or some combination. It can be about you or through the voice of a character. It can be in first person (recommended) or third person. Use lots of sensory imagery: sights, sounds, smells, etc. Use specific names of places and things.

Your song will be in verse form. It may not even need a chorus if the storytelling really engages the imagination and keeps things moving. If you do find a chorus that fits the whole story, then great, do that. A refrain is a good thing, too, if you can find a line that fits each part of the story or an image to center the whole thing around. If you do use a refrain, be aware that the word that ends it most likely will need a set-up rhyme in each verse. This is the form that Bob Dylan excels at. Have a listen to songs such as "Desolation Row," "Visions of Johanna," "Tangled Up in Blue" and "Simple Twist of Fate."

You will want at least three verses. Most likely you will not have a bridge. A bridge can get in the way in a storytelling song.

A good technique is to have each verse reveal a different point in time, like this:

Verse 1	The present moment.
Verse 2	The past: looking back, what brought you here?
Verse 3	The future: what happens next?

The song also can begin in the past and travel a linear progression through time, even if the time elapsed is very short. A story could be about any event in any life, right? Think back to a moment or event in your own life that changed you. Either begin with music by improvising words, chords and melodies that match the feeling, or "free" write all you can remember about that memory. Who, what, where, when, how... don't worry so much about the "why." Believe me, the more specific you are in your imagery, the more people will respond.

If you feel you are revealing too much or you are uncomfortable with this style of first person, autobiographical narrative, then you might want to write through a character's voice. Some people find inspiration by reading short stories, reading the news, looking at websites such as storycorps.org, or just creating characters from their imaginations. Some writers who use this technique are John Prine, Robbie Robertson (the Band), Harry Chapin, Patty Griffin, Gillian Welch, Paul Simon and many, many others.

Remember, you can tell as much of the story as you'd like. "Matty Groves," a centuries-old English folk ballad recorded by Fairport Convention in 1969, lays out the entire tragic tale of lovers killed by the noblewoman's husband. Simon's "Me and Julio Down by the Schoolyard" is a vivid story song, yet it leaves to your imagination "what the mama saw." Nick Lowe, in contrast, doesn't skimp on the details in his fanciful account of doomed folk singer "Marie Provost" (Prevost in real life), who, as the chorus states, "was a winner who became a doggie's dinner."

Whatever your story, tell it.

AABABA: Beatles Form

You're going to take the Beatles' most common template to create your own song

The lasting influence that John Lennon and Paul McCartney's song-writing has had on popular music cannot be overstated. Not only were they brilliantly gifted and creative, but many of their songs were the world's most popular songs at the time, and their catalog continues to be widely known by each new generation. They intro-duced melody, harmony and lyric ideas that are still recognizable as "Beatlesque" in songs on the charts today. Now you're going to take the Beatles' most common template — which, granted, covers a tremendous amount of stylistic ground — to create your own song.

People in class occasionally remark that because the Beatles couldn't read music, their accomplishments are that much more remarkable. The truth is that reading music has very little to do with modern pop songwriting. Reading and writing music are useful for communicating ideas and arrangements or for getting groups of musicians to play together. The Beatles, like most post-World War II popular music writers and performers, learned and communicated their ideas by ear.

In the beginning their insatiable hunger for late-1950s/early-1960s American R&B and rock 'n' roll led them to seek out these records, master the parts and perform them in seemingly endless sets night after night in Liverpool and, with particular intensity, Hamburg, Germany. Their repertoire included songs by Elvis Presley, Buddy Holly, Doc Pomus, Gerry Goffin & Carole King, Jerry Leiber & Mike Stoller, Burt Bacharach, Phil Spector, Smokey Robinson, Arthur Alexander and others. The Beatles learned how chords, melodies and song form work together by getting inside these songs, and they used that knowledge when they began writing their own material.

Lennon probably couldn't have told you that the F chord in the bridge of Buddy Holly's "Peggy Sue," or the F minor chord in Santo and Johnny's "Sleepwalk" were both borrowed from the parallel minor, but he certainly could hear it, and he used variations on that sound throughout his career. It's also important to note that McCartney's father was a musician who played in jazz bands in Liverpool. The music Paul's dad performed and listened to at home would have been in the popular form of that pre-war period: the AABA form, where each A section is a verse with a refrain, and the B section is a bridge. This, as opposed to songs with verse/chorus form, was the primary influence at a fundamental age for McCartney.

The transition from AABA to verse/chorus as the primary popular song form occurred in the 1960s. The Beatles embraced both. It may be surprising to see how many of the Beatles' songs do not have a chorus at all but rather have a refrain that begins or ends each verse, plus a bridge.

The template most often used by the Beatles, including George Harrison, is this:

Verse 1 + refrain

Verse 2 + refrain

Bridge

Verse 3 + refrain

Repeat Bridge

Repeat Verse 3 or 1

Fade or coda ending

"I Saw Her Standing There"
"A Hard Day's Night"
"I Should Have Known Better"
"And I Love Her"
"Things We Said Today"
"Yesterday"
"We Can Work It Out"
"Norwegian Wood"
"Nowhere Man"
"Michelle"
"I'm Looking Through You"
"Here, There and Everywhere"
"She Said She Said"
"Fixing a Hole"
"Lovely Rita"
"While My Guitar Gently Weeps"
"Blackbird"
"I Will"
"Hey Jude"
"Something"
"The Long and Winding Road"

There are many more. The Beatles called their bridges the middle 8, a Tin Pan Alley-era reference to an eight-measure section in the middle of the song. A bridge and a middle 8 are the same thing. Sometimes the Beatles don't repeat the bridge. Sometimes they insert an instrumental solo after the bridge. Sometimes they don't even include a refrain line in the second verse. Sometimes the ending/coda is a really memorable part, such as the "Na na na" extended fade of "Hey Jude." The Beatles were very creative within this basic template.

So that's what you're going to do with this assignment: Write a song in the Beatles' AABABA form. Listen to these songs for inspiration. Note the creativity and economy of all the elements: melody, chords, rhythm, lyrics. Most of these songs are shorter than three minutes. Make that a goal for this assignment. Even if you're not a Beatles fan, as a songwriter you must come to terms with their lasting influence and have an understanding of their work.

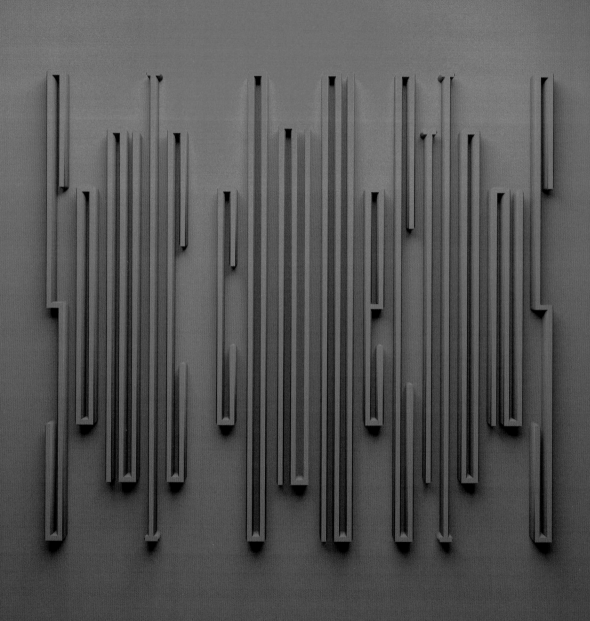

The Sound of the Words

This assignment is meant to tune your ears to the sound of the words

People say that song lyrics are not poetry, and they are correct. Lyrics are often poetic and certainly use poetic devices, but song lyrics are meant to be sung. This assignment is meant to tune your ears to the sound of the words.

When we sing we basically sing the vowels and use the consonants to shape and link them. That's a big generalization, but it's basically true. It's important to be aware of the vowel sounds you are using and how you are using them. It's also important to be aware of the consonants you are using and how they rhythmically lay out across your melody.

A well-written lyric should be easy to sing, or at least it should have an internal flowing, rhythmic logic. A poorly written lyric is often difficult to navigate and can cause all sorts of problems for the singer. I'm sure you've written lines with too many syllables or awkward consonant combinations, and when you try to sing them, they sound very unmusical. I certainly have. That's when you know it's time for some editing and rewriting.

The challenge is to write lyrics that have both meaning and musical flow. Often musical flow is more important that meaning. That doesn't let you off the hook to write meaningful words, but you can't let meaning overpower music. If the lyric is fighting the music, then the whole song is called into question. Most listeners will hear the sound of the words long before they start to put together the meaning.

I think it's a good idea to read poetry for this very reason. Don't get hung up in what the poem is "about"; just read it for the sheer joy and beauty of language. Say it out loud to yourself and be aware of how the words spill together. Or sing a song from the classic Tin Pan Alley era of songwriting. Those lyricists set the standard for musical lyric writing. My favorite is Lorenz Hart ("My Funny Valentine"), but also explore Cole Porter ("I Get a Kick Out of You"), Ira Gershwin ("Someone To Watch Over Me"), Billy Strayhorn ("Lush Life") and so many others.

The point here is...Sonic Connections

Be aware of the sounds you are making. If you make an "ooo" sound, make another "ooo" sound within the next 10 syllables. That goes for any sound that you find interesting, vowel or consonant. So if you make an "acks" sound (like "tax" or "lacks" or "packs"), make another one within the next 10 syllables. Don't worry about the meaning at all. This song should be nonsense.

Here's my example of one verse

Bring back the black mendozza (7 SYLLABLES)

Who downed the tacks and zapped the gristle (9)

Who guarded granny's garden weasel (9)

Bring him back, bring him back, bring him back (9)

Sounds used "B," "Z"/"S" connections, "acks," "D," soft "a," "G," repetition of the word "who."

Be also aware of your syllable counts and the flow of the lines. Try to give the verses matching syllable counts. That would mean line 1 of each verse in the song above will have seven syllables, while lines 2, 3 and 4 will each have nine.

Try to use some internal rhyming, as in the first line with the words "back" and "black." "Guarded" and "garden" also have a soft internal rhyme.

Write four verses of four lines, each filled with sonic connections, internal rhymes and nonsense. You can end each verse with a refrain if you like (same line ends each verse), or you can write a two-line chorus that comes between each verse. Don't let the chorus make sense of the song, though.

I think you will find that setting this lyric to music will be relatively easy. You could compose a melody and chords *first* if that makes it easier to write these lyrics.

Have fun with it.

Major to Minor and Back Again

Learn to use the chord chart to enrich the harmonic palate of your songs

Now we're really going to get to know the chord chart (pp. 116-117) and learn to use it to enrich the harmonic palate of your songs. I'd recommend having it out and available for reference the entire time you work on this song.

This song will have a verse/chorus/bridge form: three distinct sections. For the verses you'll be using chords, and corresponding melody notes, in a major key. That's the top box of the chart. Feel free to use any major key that appeals to you. Try playing through all the chords in any given key and see whether any of them sounds better than any others. Some people have emotional responses to certain keys, and others associate colors to different keys. "Flat" keys (F, Bb, Eb, Ab, Db) are often considered "dark."

An interesting historical side note: Prior to the guitar becoming the primary instrument in popular music (pre-Elvis and -British Invasion), songs were mostly written on piano and performed by groups that included horns. Without my getting into a long-winded explanation, just know that horns generally are tuned to Bb or Eb, so the majority of recorded popular music from the 1920s to the 1950s was predominantly written in the "flat" keys listed above.

When the transition to guitar-based music in the late 1950s and '60s occurred, songs and recordings started being written in guitar-friendly "sharp" keys (G, D, A, E), and that's still where we are today. The key of C major, which includes no flat or sharp notes, was and is a constant through all periods of writing. You will notice that songwriters who write on piano tend to choose from a wider palate of keys and often prefer flat keys, while guitar-based writers prefer sharp keys. If the guitar player employs a capo, though, then that changes the equation. Onward!

Your verses will be in a major key. Use the inherent musicality and drama built into the key by having climactic moments supported by the dominant chord (5th chord in the key) and resolved moments supported by the tonic chord (the 1st chord in the key.) Try to use I, IV, V along with ii, iii and vi minor.

Sample chord progression in C major:
C F Dm F Am Em G G7

Your chorus will be in the relative minor key. That is a minor key based on the 6th chord in whatever major key you are working with. Look at the chart. For the key of C major the relative minor key is A minor. Am has the same chords as C major with one *huge* exception: It includes an E major chord. That will make the Am sound like the new home base. Try it out. A great way to get from major to relative minor is to use that chord as a transition device. Here's an example:

VERSE CHORD PROGRESSION (IN MAJOR KEY)

C	F	Dm	F	Am	Em	G	G7
C	F	Dm	F	Am	Em	E	E7

CHORUS (IN RELATIVE MINOR)

Am	Am	Dm	Dm	E	E	Am	Am
Am	Am	Dm	Dm	E	E	Am	G

G chord transitions us back to the verse key (C major)
Verse 2: same chords as verse 1.
Chorus 2: same chords and words as chorus 1

Exciting, right? Now, for the super crazy icing on your fancy major/minor song, let's go to the parallel minor for a bridge.

Parallel minor is a minor key that has the same *letter* name as the major key you are working with. So for C major the parallel minor would be C minor. For A major it would be A minor. Get it?

C major and C minor have the same V (5th) chord: a G or G7. The example chorus already ends in G, so we're all set to have the bridge start on a C minor chord. It will sound very dark and ominous. Great!

EXAMPLE BRIDGE IN PARALLEL MINOR

Cm   Bb   Ab   G7   Cm   Bb   Ab   G7

At this point you have a few options on where to go form-wise. Maybe you want a big ol' guitar (or dulcimer or electric rake) solo. That could be played over any of the sections' chords. You could choose to do a third verse or repeat the first verse. Often this comes with a dynamic shift, usually a quiet passage after the build and drama of the bridge. You could choose to go right to the final chorus and repeat it several times with vigor. If that's what you want to do, you'll probably want to adjust the last chord of the bridge to an E or E7 to make a nice musical transition to the Am key.

That would look like this:

BRIDGE

Cm   Bb   Ab   G7   Cm   Bb   Ab   E7

OK, so now you have a very cool chord progression. What's next? Play through it. Maybe record it. Put it on while your do other things: washing dishes, exercising, driving, walking....Begin to sing a melody over it. Be aware that every note in each chord is a potential melody note, so if you're having trouble finding a melody, go through each chord note by note and listen for melody options.

Improvise words or non-word vowel sounds. What does the song seem to be about? What's on your mind? What do you care about? Write all that stuff down.

Here's what the example song would look like. Feel free to use this progression if you like — or use these tools to come up with you own.

VERSE 1

C   F   Dm   F   Am   Em   G   G7
C   F   Dm   F   Am   Em   E   E7

CHORUS 1

Am	Am	Dm	Dm	E	E	Am	Am
Am	Am	Dm	Dm	E	E	Am	G

VERSE 2

C	F	Dm	F	Am	Em	G	G7
C	F	Dm	F	Am	Em	E	E7

CHORUS 2

Am	Am	Dm	Dm	E	E	Am	Am
Am	Am	Dm	Dm	E	E	Am	G

BRIDGE

Cm	Bb	Ab	G7	Cm	Bb	Ab	G7

GUITAR SOLO OVER ½ VERSE

C	F	Dm	F	Am Em	E	E7

FINAL CHORUS

Am	Am	Dm	Dm	E	E	Am	Am
Am	Am	Dm	Dm	E	E	Am	G

End on Am, or repeat Chorus and fade.

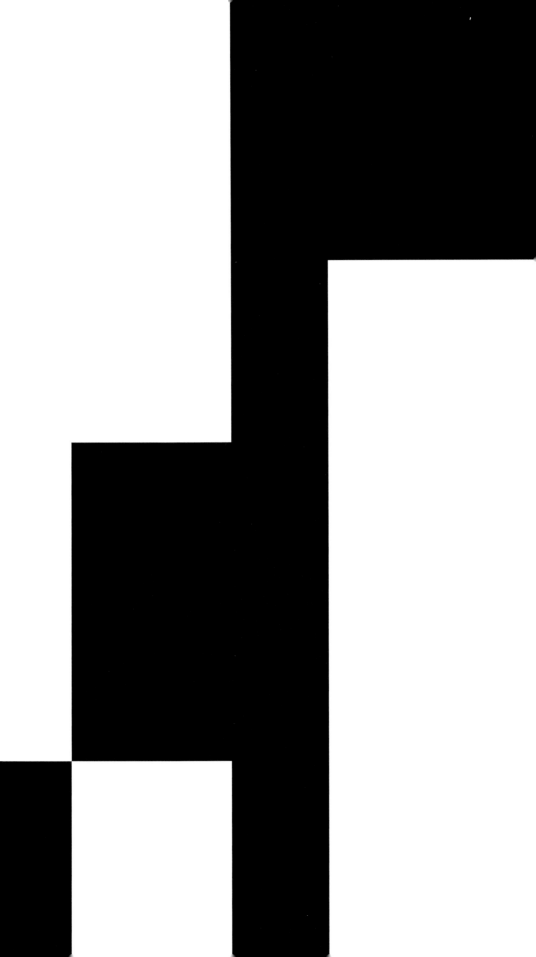

Music Is Embedded into Our Very Existence

Take the time to count the number of heartbeats between the beginning of each breath. Let that be the time signature for this song

Our bodies run on music. Our heartbeat is a persistent, rhythmic pulse that goes on day and night, constant and life-giving. Our breathing is the same; a slower rhythmic pattern. Take the time to count the number of heartbeats between the beginning of each breath. Let that be the time signature for this song.

For example: Eight heartbeats per breath will be some variation of an 8th note rhythm. A straightforward approach would be a 4/4 beat with straight 8ths — with the defining subdivision being the 8th notes. You could also do 6/8, 12/8 or, if you want a challenge, 7/8 or 9/8.

If your breath-to-heartbeat ratio is a multiple of 3, then you will write a song in waltz time or triplets (6/8, 12/8 etc.).

Your breath-to-heartbeat ratio will change depending on how relaxed you are. That's your tempo. You can manipulate this as you like. A fast song aims to increase the heartbeat and breathing of the listener. A slow song aims to calm the listener. This is a giant generalization, of course, but on a very primitive level it is true. This is communication on a primal level. Music speaks to ancient parts of our selves, as well as to highly evolved parts. This assignment is to get in touch with and become expressive with the primal part of our humanity.

When we walk, run, exercise, chew, etc, we are engaging in rhythmic pattern activity. Did you know that the pumping of blood goes right past our ears as it feeds our brains with blood? The sound of that is very loud, but our brains have learned to tune it out as "nonessential" information. But it is there every moment of every day we are alive. If you've ever had an ear infection, you know that sound because it throws the brain off, and we become aware of the sound.

Now consider the world around you, and open your mind to the idea that every single sound you hear is musical: birds, cars, the wind, your cell phone, the tapping of your fingers on a computer keyboard, the voice of your best friend, your own voice talking to a pet or a new baby. There are melodic elements in all of these sounds. Become aware of the pitch and timbre of all sounds. Try to bring one of more of these elements into your melody.

OK, so use your own heartbeat and breathing to create a rhythmic underpinning for your song. Use sounds of the world around you to create a melody for your song. Form and lyrics are completely up to you.

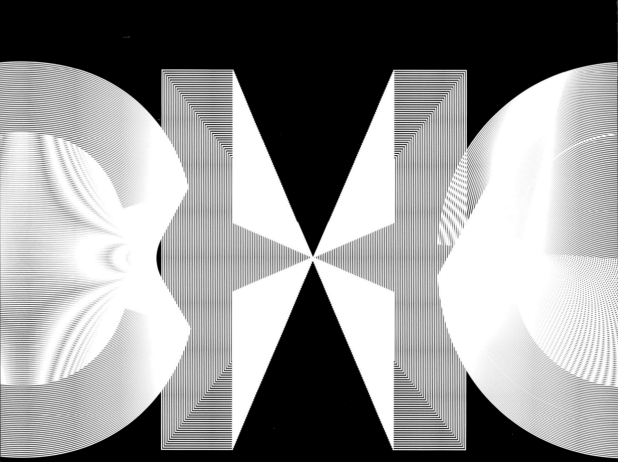

Fancy chords

You're going to create a compound chord bank using the parallel minor, and then you'll use those chords to create a chord progression that weaves through multiple keys

As noted in Assignment 8, parallel minor is the key that has the same letter name as its major-key partner. For example, the parallel minor for G major is G minor. Let's write out all the chords in those two keys:

G major	G	Am	Bm	C	D	Em	F#dim
G minor	Gm	Adim	Bb	Cm	Dm	Eb	F

Now we'll combine them to make a compound chord bank:

G Gm Am Adim Bb Bm C Cm D Dm Eb Em F F#dim

Next I will make a progression incorporating chords from this chord bank using *root motion* as the linking device. Root motion in 4th's and whole or half steps always works.

G	Bm	Bb	Eb	Em	Am	Dm	Dm
Gm	F	Em	D	G	Bb	Eb	D

Because the chords are all derived from G or G minor, there are common notes that will work over most of the chords: the tonic (a G) and the fifth (a D). Try singing a G or D note over the entire progression. In the above progression, a D note will work over the nearly all of it.

The Beatles used this technique liberally, as did post-Beatles bands such as Squeeze and Crowded House in songs such as "Tempted" and "Four Seasons in One Day," respectively. It is also found in pre-rock standards ("Smoke Gets In Your Eyes," "Darn That Dream," "Have You Met Miss Jones") and songs by Burt Bacharach and Hal David ("What's New Pussycat?" "What the World Needs Now," "Anyone Who Had A Heart") and others.

Make your own chord bank, or use the one created here, and then write a song using complex chords.

Got it?

Good.

Root Motion and the Line of 4ths

We're going to look at the Line of 4ths chart, talk about how it applies to composing chord progressions and write a song that incorporates this cool, if complex, concept

When we are learning music theory and key signatures, we talk about the Circle of 5ths, a round diagram that arranges keys in Perfect 5th intervals clockwise. It can be a great learning tool, but I found that trying to use it in classes where people had little or no music theory knowledge just made things more confusing. I realized that most of my students were guitar players and that the low strings of a guitar in standard tuning are tuned in 4ths. Aha! So they already know a series of notes in 4ths — E A D G — without even realizing.

So then I thought about creating a "line of 4ths" that expands through all 12 tones from the G until it reaches the next E:

E A D G C F Bb Eb Ab Db Gb B E
The line of 4ths!

Why 4ths? I don't know why we love the sound of chords moving with root motion in 4ths, but we do. It is probably a combination of the physics and mathematics of sound and overtones and cultural conditioning. Root motion in 4ths goes back to Bach, probably before that even. So what is root motion? What are we talking about here?

The root is the note that the chord is named for. It is the note the bass player usually will play on the downbeat of a new chord. It defines, anchors and creates context for everything else musically. The root of a C chord is a C. The root of a Cm7(b5) chord is a C. The root of a C#dim7 is a C#. The root of an Am7 is an A. Get it?

Roots love to move along in 4ths. You kind of can't go wrong if you create a chord progression that has root motion moving in 4ths. Here's a basic and common chord progression in the key of C using root motion in 4ths:

C   Am   Dm   G   C

Look at the line above and you'll see A D G C all next to each other on the line. Nifty!

So that's all fine, but what about using root motion in 4ths to bring in chords and sounds from outside of the key? This is a great idea. Let's take the progression above and spice it up a bit:

C   A7   Dm   G

The A7 chord adds a C# note to the musical palette and thus some tension and drama. The C# adds what we call a "leading tone" into the mix. C# is one half step away from the D in the D minor chord. In a way the A7 becomes the "personal" dominant chord of the D minor. In proper music theory, this is called a secondary dominant or a V of ii.

I like the term "personal" dominant chord. It's more approachable. So get this: *Any* chord can have a personal dominant chord, and to find it all you have to do is look at the line of 4ths. Find the root of the chord you want your chord progression to go to on the line. Then, to find that chord's personal dominant chord, find the note immediately to the left of that root. Then make that into a dominant 7th chord. Here are a few examples:

Target chord is C minor. Root = C. Preceding C on the line of 4ths is G. Make G into G7.

G7 is the personal dominant chord of C minor. Actually G7 is the personal dominant chord of *any* chord that has C as its root.

Target chord is Fmaj7. Root = F. Preceding F on the line of 4ths is C. Make C into C7.

C7 is the personal dominant chord of Fmaj7.

C A7 Dm G7 C C7 Fmaj7 G7 Cm G7 Cm A7 Dm G7 C

Many, many songs from America's musical history use dominant chords (7th chords, like G7 or A7) moving in 4ths. Listen to "I Got Rhythm," "Bill Bailey," "Nobody Knows You When You're Down and Out," "On The Sunny Side of the Street" "Love Me Tender" and "Salty Dog Blues." There are literally thousands of them. At key points in the songs, they all use a cycle of dominant chords moving in 4ths, like this:

D7   G7   C7   F7

This particular cycle is from the bridge of "I Got Rhythm" by George and Ira Gershwin. The verses use another cycle of 4ths, the I vi ii V cycle first mentioned above. These patterns are so often used in composition, they are simply referred to as "Rhythm changes" in reference to that archetypal song.

Rhythm changes in Bb

Verses	Bb	Gm	Cm	F7
Bridge	D7	G7	C7	F7

Note then that the quality of the chord (major, minor, dominant) is adjustable as long as the root motion moves in a logical 4ths pattern. This is great news because it gives you lots of options.

You now have one more excellent compositional tool: Root motion in 4ths *always* works and draws upon hundreds of years of tried and true musical knowledge. Sweet.

One more thing: In addition to root motion in 4ths, roots love to move in whole and half steps. Think of the roots of your chords as chess pieces that have certain specific, allowable moves. OK, that sounds too much like a strict rule, and I hate strict rules in songwriting. Think of them as *suggested* moves. That's better.

Here are the suggested root moves from a C chord

C to F (root motion up a 4th, from the line of 4ths)

C to D (up a step)

C to B (down a half step)

C to C# (up a half step)

This will be tricky, but let's use all four examples in one progression. Remember it is just root motion, so I can "color" the chords any way I like.

Cmaj7 Fmaj7 Cmaj7 Dm Cmaj7 G/B C A/C# Dm G Cmaj7

OK, that was sneaky but important. I used *inversions* (G/B and A/C#) to get the half step bass motion. Inversions are when you put a note other than the root of the chord in the bass. Inversions are easier to play on piano, but certain ones sit well on guitar, too. Fleetwood Mac's "Landslide" has this chord progression:

C G/B Am7 G/B
(with the guitar capo'd at the 3rd fret on the recording)

So we have bass motion of a half step (C to B) and a whole step (B to A), along with voice leading and movement from major to minor. Nice, simple and effective.

Now you are going to write a song that uses these techniques. Use some root motion in 4ths. Try to get outside the key somewhere in the song by using the personal dominant chord technique. That will create some nice tension. Also try to use an inversion or two to utilize bass motion in whole or half steps.

This is advanced, tricky stuff yet not as hard as it sounds, and it's very, very useful and effective.

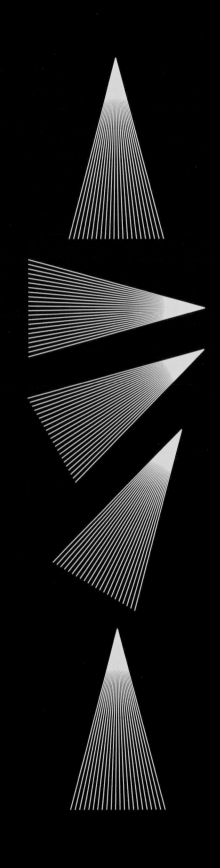

In The Style of…

You're going to write songs in the style of other artists and songwriters

Every session in my Old Town School of Folk Music classes, I try to give one assignment that requires students to research and explore the work of influential songwriters from the past. I've had good luck with students writing in the style of Buddy Holly, John Lennon and Roy Orbison.

More recently I've been giving assignments based on the fact that songwriters, in many cases, were behind-the-scenes artisans working on crafting songs for popular singers. This, I think, is a good way to get to know the work of great writers who aren't necessarily performers and to have a better understanding of the history of songwriting. Those assignments have included songs written as if for Elvis Presley (circa 1968), Linda Ronstadt (1973) and the big one, Frank Sinatra.

Now you're going to write songs in the style of other artists and songwriters.

Turn the page to find three to do.

Patsy Cline

It is 1961. You're a struggling songwriter living in Nashville. You're having a few cocktails in a bar one lonely night, and you strike up a conversation with some guy who's having a beer. After a exchanging pleasantries, he tells you he's Randy Hughes, Patsy Cline's manager, and he's having a difficult time finding a follow-up to Patsy's last big hit, Hank Cochran's, "I Fall To Pieces." When you tell him you're a songwriter, he says, "Come on by the office next week and play me some of your songs."

This is your big chance. Write the song you're going to play for Randy Hughes

To prepare: Listen to Patsy Cline's songs and figure out what she does.

"Crazy" (written by Willie Nelson)
"I Fall To Pieces" (Hank Cochran and Harlan Howard)
"Walking After Midnight" (Alan Block and Donn Hecht)
"Sweet Dreams" (Don Gibson)
"She's Got You" (Cochran)
"Leavin' on your Mind" (Wayne Walker and Webb Pierce)
"Imagine That" (Justin Tubb)

Patsy Cline's big hits were primarily ballads with expressive melodies that showcased her range and expressiveness. Nearly *all* of her hits feature the title of the song as the opening line, as a refrain, so no chorus is needed on your song for Patsy.

The form will probably be

Verse 1	with refrain as opening line
Verse 2	same chords, melody as verse one
Bridge	Simple bridge, probably beginning on the IV chord of the key
Repeat	Verse 1 or new Verse 3 with refrain

It is 1965, and you are a songwriter living in New York City. Don Kirshner calls you and says he needs songs for a TV show about a Beatles-inspired band called the Monkees. The songs need to be upbeat, fun and catchy with jangly guitars and vocal harmonies. They can't be longer than three minutes. If you place a song on the TV show, it'll be on the corresponding album, and that's double the royalties. You need this! Write the song you will present to Don Kirshner.

Explore the Monkees catalog and become familiar with what similarities there might be. What is the subject matter? Here are some of their biggest songs:

"Last Train To Clarksville" (Tommy Boyce-Bobby Hart): fast tempo, great guitar riff, cool vocal hooks ("oh, no, no, no"), subject is a love song of sorts; singer needs to see his girlfriend one last time. Length: 2:44. Key: G major.

"I'm a Believer" (Neil Diamond): up-tempo love song with cool organ and guitar hooks and an irresistible sing-along chorus. Length: 2:50. Key: G major.

"(I'm Not Your) Steppin' Stone" (Boyce-Hart): bluesy up-tempo song with an indelible vocal/harmonic riff ("I-I-I-I'm not your stepping store"). Unusual in that it goes into double-time, has a drum break also boasts an angry narrative. Length: 2:23. Recurring chord pattern: E G A C, which means it is not squarely in a key; it is an E blues-based riff song.

"Daydream Believer" (John Stewart): Three minutes of pure pop candy driven by an insistent quarter-note piano and a backbeat. It's more of a solo piece for Davy Jones than a group song. I have no idea what it's about beyond waking up in the morning. Maybe that's it. Maybe it doesn't matter. Length: 2:54. Key: F major.

Explore others ("Porpoise Song," anyone?) and write a hit for the Monkees

Max Martin

You're a protégé of Max Martin, the Swedish songwriter who has written or co-written the third most No. 1 songs after Paul McCartney and John Lennon. His first chart-topper was Britney Spears' "...Baby One More Time," and others include Katy Perry's "I Kissed a Girl," "Teenage Dream" and "Roar" and Taylor Swift's "We Are Never Ever Getting Back Together," "Shake It Off" and "Bad Blood" — and he also co-wrote Adele's "Send My Love (To Your New Lover)."

Anyway, Max tells you that he needs a song for a hot new artist, but he's too deeply entrenched in his latest megastar project to give it the proper effort. Could you take care of this, please?

Here's what this song needs:

A danceable, hand-clap-able rhythm — often the song's starting point.

A big earworm chorus that prominently features the title and could be sung by multiple (or multitracked) voices.

A verse-chorus-verse-chorus-bridge-chorus structure — but consider throwing in some pre-choruses too.

An attitude of empowerment.

Words that sound good together but don't necessarily make complete sense.

Now go write that song that will make the whole world sing along, whether they want to or not.

Up Above My Head, I Hear Music in the Air…

You are going to write a song in your head

Finally, you are going to write a song in your head. No instrument, no pen, no paper, no Voice Memo recording. It will exist only in your imagination and memory until it is set in a semi-finished state. You will find this very difficult and very rewarding. It is my contention that you already know everything you need to know about songwriting and that you just need to get out of your own way. This is one way to work on getting out of your own way.

We can focus on the craft elements of songwriting forever, and they will make you understand elements of music and songcraft better, but songs are best when they come from the heart and soul. You want to be in dialogue with yourself and the music that moves *you*, and you want to let go of trying to sound like something that already exists (or trying *not* to sound like something that already exists) and any notions of "rules."

Start by spending time in a place that is very quiet and where no music can be heard. Take some time to clear your mind. Try listening to your breath, counting how many heartbeats are in each breath, or any meditation practice you like.

Next, imagine a song. Let it play in your mind and try to listen to it rather than force it into being. Try to get a "big picture" view. Listen for the overall feeling and effect it has on you, and try to conjure and recall what it sounds like.

Things to listen for:

Tempo	Fast, slow, medium?
Meter	4/4, 3/4, straight or swing feel?
Dynamics	Loud, soft, combination?
Overall feeling	Joy, sadness, longing, angry, excited?
Chords	Simple? Complex? In one key or multiple keys? Major or Minor? Combination?
Melody	High? Low? Active (a lot of notes and a big range)? Passive (fewer notes and small range)?
Form	Is there a chorus? A bridge? Are there many verses?
Lyrics	Are there words? Any phrases that repeat or jump out at you?

Probably not all of these questions will be answered at first. They may also sway what you are hearing. Try to hear as much of the song in your head as you can before you try to answer these questions. As you attempt to answer them, the song should begin to become more focused. At that point it is time to begin crafting the song in your head.

The next step is actively to try out words, phrases and melodies. You can sing them aloud, but don't write them down or record them. You'll have to repeat it to yourself often to retain it. This is good for you.

Once you have a basic form, lyrics, and melody, you can write them down and start trying to find the chords you heard in your head. It may be a good idea at this point to make a memo recording of the melody and words in their original state, as adding chords will most likely change the song.

MARK   This is the first way I ever "wrote," and I continue to do so, often when I'm not expecting to. My chief variation from what Steve suggested is this: I'm almost always in motion when I write in my head. I've come up with numerous melodies and other musical ideas while riding my bike or walking to the train or swimming or driving (with the radio off). I may be clearing my mind during these activities, but I'm not blocking out the outside world. In ways I couldn't begin to pinpoint, the rotation of the wheels or the insistence of my steps or the backdrop of the breeze or traffic provides a foundation and often a rhythm.

Sometimes a phrase pops into my head (one bleak, snowy walk triggered "I feel like a park in the winter") with a melody attached. Sometimes it's just a tune or a beat. Whatever comes first I try to "listen" for what comes next. I play that snippet in my head over and over, trying to push it to the next logical part. If it feels like a chorus, what does the transition to the verse sound like? How does the verse go? If what comes first feels like a verse, let's try to get it to the chorus or maybe a bridge. Just keep replaying the thing, trying to move the ball a bit farther forward while cementing what's there in your head. (I realize there's a ball and cement in there, but this is tricky business.)

Once I have something that feels like a legitimate song chunk, something upon which I can build, I'll record it. My voicemail at work used to be filled with recordings of me making mouth percussion noises while humming out a melody, perhaps with a few phrases thrown in. It's important to record what you've got in some recognizable form because it's easy to forget what you've concocted even if you've repeated it in your head 100 times. Think of all the great songs lost in the fog of memory…

The next step, as Steve mentioned, is to figure out the song on an instrument. I usually pull out my guitar and try to find the chords that I'm hearing in my head. Sometimes I think: Oh, that turned out to be pretty simple. Other times I think: Hey, that's a pretty cool change right there. It's best not to judge these things, of course, and there's often more than one answer regarding which chord fits at a given moment, but usually there's a "right" one that I've been hearing — and fingers crossed that I'm capable of playing it. I'm likely to finish the song on the instrument, but then again, I've often come up with bridges for long-dormant songs when out on another bike ride. Having your music on auto-play in your head will keep those wheels turning.

One more thought: The idea of writing in your head may sound intimidating, but consider this: Every time you open your mouth, you're improvising what comes out of it. Neither you nor anybody else pre-scripts everything you say. You're choosing words and phrasings, and there's a rhythm and melody to how you talk, so your ability to make things up on the spot is a native one. Try singing instead of talking, and you may be surprised how quickly you can "compose."

Anyone can do this, after all.

Final Thought

Congratulations for making it to the end of the book! We hope you've found it helpful and it has given you inspiration to continue your own creative pursuits. Now, a final thought:

We are all too busy, and songwriting is hard. So why bother?

Creating music makes you a better person. Engaging in any type of music-making causes you to open your senses, to focus your attention and to work on something that may be slow and difficult but worthwhile. In those rare moments when it all comes together and the music seems to flow through you, you feel a sense of accomplishment and joy that is deep and real. This focus and feeling of satisfaction will begin to show up in other parts of your life as well.

Writing songs engages all parts of your brain. Singing original songs engages all parts of your brain and much of your physical body. Creative expression is good for you and good for the universe.

Meanwhile, we live in a fast-moving, cynical world that often views music-making and other forms of creative expression as a means to riches, fame and glory. We relate through digitally transmitted fragments, snapshots and other communicative shortcuts. True, meaningful expression can be frowned upon, called "cheesy," considered too time consuming to offer or to digest. Our sense of separation from our fellow humans is profound and growing.

But expressing yourself and searching for your truths and motivations makes you a more empathetic person and releases compassionate energy into the universe. By sharing your thoughts, insights, experiences, joys, sorrows and loves with the world, you are proclaiming your humanness, breaking down the barriers and offering points of powerful connection. That in turn can encourage others to do the same. This is true whether you're issuing albums on major labels, performing on stages large or small, or posting a song that three people will hear online.

And remember: When songwriting works — when you land upon a song that really hits the mark — there is no better feeling.

Thanks for reading, and please stop by our website, tothebridgebook. com, where you can interact with us and other songwriters and share the songs that spring from these assignments. We can't wait to experience the positive musical energy that you add to the universe.

Steve and Mark

ABOUT THE AUTHORS

Steve Dawson has been writing songs for more than 30 years, most prominently as leader of the band Dolly Varden, which has released six acclaimed studio albums and toured the U.S. and Europe. He also has written and recorded two solo albums; a duets album with his wife, Dolly Varden bandmate/visual artist Diane Christiansen; and an album with three of Chicago's most revered improvising musicians in a band called Funeral Bonsai Wedding. Since 2006 he has taught songwriting classes at Chicago's legendary Old Town School of Folk Music. At his recording studio, Kernel Sound Emporium, he has produced more than two dozen albums by up-and-coming songwriters.

Mark Caro is author of *The Foie Gras Wars* (Simon & Schuster), which won the 2009 Great Lakes Book Award for general nonfiction and two prizes from the Gourmand World Cookbook Awards in Paris. For more than 25 years, he wrote about music, film, food and other cultural topics for the *Chicago Tribune*, and he since has written for The *New York Times* and other publications. He also created and hosts the popular "Is It Still Funny?" film series in Chicago. He lives in the Chicago area with his wife, radio personality Mary Dixon, and their two daughters.

ACKNOWLEDGMENTS

Steve and Mark would like to thank: Diane Christiansen, Mary Dixon; Evangeline Dawson; Ruth and Madeline Caro; Neville Christiansen Dawson; the entire Old Town School of Folk Music community, including Jimmy Tomasello, Charles Kim, Shelley Miller, Sue Demel and Bau Graves and all of the amazingly talented people who've taken Steve's classes over the years; Alec Harris, Tom Hawley and the good people at GIA; Bud Rodecker, Zach Minnich, Rick Valicenti and the rest of the Thirst team; Todd Rosenberg ; Phil Angotti and Avenue N Guitars; Jenny Bienemann; Ellen Cherry; Pat Byrnes; Lou Carlozo; Jen Coyle; Jonathan Eig; Paul Erickson; Ross Freedman; James Finn Garner; Perry Gattegno; Jimmy Guterman; Larry Kart; Martin Kastner; Jim Powers; Justin Roberts; Jeff Ruby; Heidi Serwer; Stuart Shea; Robert Shepard; Freda Love Smith; and all of the songwriters whose music we have loved.